**Email Marketing
for Complex Sales Cycles**

Email
MARKETING
for Complex Sales Cycles

Proven Ways
to Produce a
Continuous Flow
of Prospects and
Profits with
Effective,
Spam-Free
Email Systems

Winton Churchill

Foreword by Ron Richards – *President, ResultsLab*®

New York

Email Marketing
for Complex Sales Cycles

*Proven Ways to Produce a Continuous Flow of
Prospects and Profits with Effective, Spam-Free
Email Systems*

by Winton Churchill

ISBN 978-1-60037-421-0 Paperback
ISBN 978-1-60037-422-7 Hardcover
Library of Congress Control Number: 2008922482

Published by:

MORGAN · JAMES
THE ENTREPRENEURIAL PUBLISHER™
www.morganjamespublishing.com

Morgan James Publishing, LLC
1225 Franklin Ave. Ste 325
Garden City, NY 11530-1693
Toll Free 800-485-4943
www.MorganJamesPublishing.com

Habitat
for Humanity®
Peninsula
Building Partner

Persuasion Design® and ResultsLab® are service marks of ResultsLab.
Churchill Method™ is a trademark of Churchill Method, Inc.

This book is dedicated to those individuals with

the vision to see possibilities...

the courage to take risks...

the determination to overcome odds...

the creativity to make something out of nothing...

Contents

Chapter 2. Change Your Mindset, Change Your Future

Chapter 3. Six Special Needs of Complex Sales Cycles

Chapter 4. The Disappointment of Email Marketing

Don't Miss Out

To receive the special bonus content associated with this book that will help you implement the ideas and concepts discussed, please send an email to:

ultimate@YourBonusContent.com

Get quantity discounts

This book is available at a quantity discounts for orders of ten or more copies. Please call me toll-free at (877) 886-6256 or email me at books@YourBonusContent.com

Host a reading group

For tips on how to form and carry on a book reading group in your workplace or community, send an email to group@YourBonusContent.com.

Ask a question/read answers

If you're a thinking person, you probably have a few questions or things you are unclear about. That's OK. It's a lot to learn.

Send your questions to:

questions@YourBonusContent.com

I'll do my best to answer them on a monthly basis... I'll send you any other questions that come from your fellow readers.

Foreword

by Ron Richards, President, ResultsLab

This book is a marketing masterpiece written by a marketing genius. It's a *complete integrated system* for accomplishing things few know are possible.

Imagine being able to target your most desired prospects, by title, industry, size of company, region of the country, and what they read — and catch them early, as they enter their window of need.

Imagine all the mechanics handled for you so your emailings are welcomed as a gift of know-how, not seen as spam.

Imagine your sales people freed from numbing cold calling, spending their time instead with qualified prospects who have already learned, and agreed, that they have a burning problem — prospects eager to hear about your offering as the best solution.

Imagine your automated series of emailings keeping up the momentum at ideal intervals, with no risk of someone dropping the ball — producing a steady and predictable flow of those qualified prospects. All with you able to turn the quantity of prospects up or down, at your discretion.

How did Winton Churchill invent this system that makes all that predictable and reliable — culminating in his now having developed over 1000 emailings for his clients?

He knew the need for it because he was a star salesperson, then star sales manager, then VP Marketing in a number of highly regarded high tech companies with complex sales cycles.

I watched Winton's inventive mind build this breakthrough know-how during the 10 years he hired me to do 12 consulting projects for him. In a way, we became each other's mentors.

Many of my biggest breakthrough approaches — keys to super ROI marketing — are built into Winton's system: How to use a *learning-oriented approach* instead of selling. How to become your prospect's trusted *objective, unbiased advisor.* How to show the prospect that there is a better, *rational decision standard, under which your product is the winner and all competitors are disqualified.* How to use *grabbers* (headlines, subheads, and pictures) to create high curiosity and carry your positioning.

Winton is super-sensitive to my concepts of *the multiplier principle* and *poison elements* — the idea that if you do nine things well and only one poorly, the net result can be zero results. And if you had fixed that one thing, your results could be world class!

Indeed, Winton is sensitive to many counter-intuitive killers. For example, in one project of mine my client had massively advertised online. So virtually everyone they exposed had decided about them. I had the new advertising omit their name and logo, and come from a *news story of unique results.* That version beat the control that had taken them public — by two fold. Objective advice and curiosity sometimes trump branding.

To my thinking, this highly strategic book is a must-read if you have a complex sales cycle. It delivers a complete, integrated, profit-multiplying system to you on a silver platter.

Indeed, it may be the *only* book on emailing that's entirely dedicated to those with a complex sales cycle, with its very different requirements. And as Winton says, "The whole thing can run off into the ditch if you don't do it right."

This proven system does more than maximize your success. It also has built-in methods for you to sort your prospects by degree of interest. Yes, it's possible for your sales people to have multiples more return on their time — by spending it on pre-sold prospects at their ideal readiness moment.

The book is free from jargon and the technical information that bogs down other books. Its unique style and graphics demonstrate an approach you can use in your emailings to ensure easy reading.

And because Winton has "done it all," and knows all the essential elements and steps, he tells you the optimum number of emails to send, at what intervals; he lists sources to use (and avoid); he suggest the structure of a grabbing Subject line; and alerts you to other vital success details. It's a wonderful blend of strategic and specific.

Winton even solves the problem of closing influencer and decision groups, through his concept of a Champion Kit you can build for your prospect.

Heaven help your competitors doing conventional, shrill selling while you are educating your prospects and becoming their trusted advisor using this system. In your early emailings to them, you won't be seen as selling at all. The degree to which the book recommends this may amaze you.

And heaven help your competitors' economics as their sales people spin their wheels making dozens of calls to connect with only a few prospects — getting burned out in the process. All the while, your system delivers up to your sales people only those who are a good fit, whose actions have acknowledged a burning need. Your people are "invited in" because their credibility and expertise was already established by your emailings.

Here's to your profitability, growth, and competitive dominance using these breakthrough methods.

Ron Richards
President, ResultsLab

Acknowledgements

In acknowledging those who made this book possible, I'm reminded of the story of the turtle that woke up one morning and found himself sitting atop a fencepost.

"Hmm," he said. "I'm not sure how I got here, but I know I didn't do it alone…"

That pretty much sums it up for me as well.

I believe most people think the hardest part of publishing a book is simply writing it. It IS a daunting task to sit down at a keyboard and "plink away" until you have something you hope people will find informative and interesting.

But the fact that this book ever made it into print is less a tribute to the author than it is to the people who acted as guides down a road I traveled without a map.

My advisor, confidant and counsel George McKenzie has provided great and valuable input, insight and impetus to this work and I am grateful for his wisdom and patience.

Dr. Debi Yohn has provided clarity and perspective that I think make this work much more approachable than the early drafts.

My editor and book designer, Aaron Wrixon, from Ontario, Canada, not only lent his sharp eye to the sometimes hurried text and created a great cover, but did so (with incredibly good humor) under tight deadline pressure on several occasions. Besides being invaluable in catching "fat-fingered errors" in the copy, he often acted as a mentor as I muddled through decisions regarding layout, print, and paper.

And Demetria Wallace of Office Technology Global Business Solutions in Long Beach, California, provided quick, accurate transcriptions of interviews and teleseminars.

And lastly, my three associates I can always count on to give my work a "cat scan-like" review: Paulina, Gelsimina and Max.

In sum, I am grateful to them for helping make this book a reality. Without their talents and skills I would have never been able to reach the top of this particular fencepost.

A Personal Note About the Style of this Book
from Winton Churchill

After spending years of reading (and in some cases writing) dreadfully boring technical documents and white papers, I thought there must be a better way to communicate complex information in a more entertaining and memorable way.

As Vice President of Marketing at two major software firms, I spoke to hundreds of prospects (maybe thousands… if you count trade shows). They were the consumers of the marketing, advertising and technical literature my staff and I churned out.

As I received more and more feedback through the years from my audiences, I realized something disheartening but critically important.

First of all, much of what is written never gets read… 90% of book buyers never go past the first chapter.

And guess what else?

Even those who do get read beyond Chapter 1 don't continue straight through to the end. They often flip along, reading a section here, a page there.

I also became convinced that — worst of all — few people remember more than 10% of what they read a day later.

So I began looking for some answers and learned that there are two forms of writing. There's a more formal, even scholarly, style of writing that impresses (but is rarely read).

And there's a style of writing that is highly readable (almost conversational) and is more frequently remembered.

I began experimenting with the latter... and was pleasantly surprised by the increase in favorable comments from readers. They also seemed to be retaining more of what I wrote... and I — then and there — forever abandoned the formal style.

I was content with the results for about 10 years... until I ran across a remarkable book by Robert E. Horn, *Visual Language: Global Communication for the 21st Century*... and my style took yet another turn.

It turns out that words combined with graphics had a powerful effect on the brain's ability to plow through and retain information...

Again my audiences seemed to appreciate the change and enjoy "the ride" even more.

So, what lies ahead are not the mental ramblings of a delusional "clip artist"... but a document designed to help you enjoy, retain and benefit more from your reading investment.

Enjoy!

Introduction

Email Marketing Is Not About "Spam"

Who among us hasn't been savaged by the onslaught of "spam" — unsolicited commercial email? It fills up our mailbox and clogs our hard drives with frustrating offers of everything from miracle drugs to instant debt relief.

Being swamped by spam is like the proverbial "death by a thousand paper cuts" — sapping your energy, obscuring the important and valuable information you used to appreciate in your mailbox.

Yet, as frustrated as we all are with that, not a week goes by that I don't hear from a prospective client: "We don't market through email because we don't believe in spamming. And besides, spamming is illegal."

In the chapters that follow you'll learn the difference between spam — which is now illegal — and legitimate email marketing, which is often misunderstood and almost universally overlooked by those with complex sales cycles.

The passage of the "Controlling the Assault of Non-Solicited Pornography and Marketing Act of 2003," or CAN-SPAM Act, greatly simplified the patch work of 35+ state laws that legitimate emailers had been wrestling with in their attempts to communicate with their customers and prospects.

What can you do? There won't be a clear cut legal answer to every question. But here are some things that will make you more knowledgeable when you do go to see your legal professional.

For now, we'll all be living in this world of unsolicited email because there won't be one legal or technological solution to control it in the short-term.

Email: No "hall pass" needed

80% to 90% of spam comes from a relatively small number of spammers... they literally send millions of emails per day. And those people are very good at "cloaking" or hiding their identity (which is now officially illegal).

They're very hard to track down. Not only that, but their servers are located in places where US authorities have little influence — and zero jurisdiction... so while anti-spam laws will provide some reduction in spam and some comfort to the spam-weary... in all likelihood the flood of objectionable spam will continue.

It will take several refinements in the laws and the enforcement practices to effectively reduce spam.

Surviving the anti-spam hysteria — six realistic coping strategies

How do you cope with changing laws, spam filters, and angry email recipients who don't remember they actually asked for your information but report it as spam the instant it hits their inbox?

You must attack this problem from 6 specific angles:

Understand the "permission continuum" and use it wisely

On the right, a signed document that says "yes, you may send me email." On the left is a popup that says, "You have won a free flashlight.

Put in your email address and we'll send it to you." That email address is then sold to dozens or even hundreds of organizations.

There's "opt-in email," and then there's "relevant opt-in email." And that's a key distinction in understanding whether your permission is going to be valid or not.

The distinction between one-step marketing and two-step marketing has become blurred by the invention of email and autoresponders. Most autoresponders are one-step.

The danger of using autoresponders? Messages become increasingly shrill. The sell becomes harder with each succeeding email. The first email is a pitch. Three days later there's another pitch. Three days later, there's a special offer pitch. Three days later, you get an email saying "What's wrong? I'm confused and disappointed. Why didn't you buy this?" Another email follows that might even include insults or intimidation.

Focus on quality and value of the material you email to your prospects

- Tone: connect with prospects—"How can I help you? What problem can I help you solve?"
- Quality of content: high value to the prospect—give them enough to want more (more layers of abilities and opportunities to solve that problem)
- Quantity: High percentage of education vs. sales

Catalog carefully

Take pains to document your "permissions." Know how to find your opt-ins quickly and be prepared to prove you acquired their addresses legally.

Store systematically

Don't let one person maintain the record of permissions in one place. He or she may leave someday and you won't be able to find files when you need them. Treat this data as extremely valuable, because it could save you from a lawsuit or fine. Make sure it's accessible. A financial predator looking for a quick buck through a legal settlement will drop the case as soon as it looks questionable. Like all predators, they'll seek the easiest target.

Be careful of buying lists from third parties

Here's where the 'relevancy" test becomes critical.

For instance, if a chemical engineer subscribes to an industry publication, and agrees to look at information relevant to chemical engineering, you're going to (probably) be safe.

However, if you bought the email address from someone promoting a contest or a sweepstakes, and the recipient hasn't specifically expressed an interest in your subject... look out.

Look at offline lead generation

People have become so sick of spam that traditional, "low-tech" offline marketing methods are enjoying a resurgence.

Since email came along, people are getting less and less paper correspondence. When something does arrive in their mailbox, it's almost become a treat. As hard as it is to believe, junk mail isn't such junk anymore.

We'll open an envelope out of curiosity. We'll read a well-done postcard as we walk back to our house after we take it out of the mailbox.

But our email inbox gets so cluttered with spam that we often get into a deleting frenzy. Have you ever accidentally deleted an email you wanted to read along with the dozens of others you didn't — just because you were hitting the delete key so furiously you trashed something you shouldn't have?

As a result, offline methods like direct mail have begun to convert prospects to buyers at a higher, more profitable percentage than you might expect.

What's going to happen now?

For all the good intentions in the new laws, there will probably continue to be a large amount of spam finding its way onto your computer every day.

And once people — especially lawmakers — realize that the quick fix approaches we've seen so far won't work, there will be a second wave of technology and legislation that will go a long way toward correcting the problem. There will be progress in shutting down the true spammers, who are relatively few in number.

Once they're gone, legitimate email marketers will see increased opportunities because email will become relevant again.

Five simple steps you can take to put spammers out of business

The sooner spam goes away, the more legitimate businesses can begin to use email as an effective and profitable marketing strategy.

Here are 5 steps you can personally take to hasten the day it happens.

1. Never buy products from spammers. Every sale they make encourages them to keep doing it. No one stays in business for long if nobody's buying anything from them.
2. Support your local "spam sheriffs." Actively and persistently encourage lawmakers — in writing — to enact legislation that strikes at the heart of spam rather than "feel good" regulations that get lots of publicity but little in the way of results. Beware of sweeping legislation that is poorly crafted. It can hurt legitimate businesses and increase compliance costs.
3. Follow scrupulous "permission" guidelines yourself. Be absolutely certain you have permission to do your mailings.
4. Be authentically interested in serving your client's interest and not

just selling them something. Find ways to inform and educate them in a manner that leads them to want to do business with you.

5. Resist the temptation to "take advantage" of a list that you are not absolutely sure conveys permission for your mailing.

It's critical that you know both the spirit and the letter of the law when preparing your email marketing campaigns and your email documents.

I recommend that you do rigorous research, consult with a knowledgeable attorney, and conscientiously follow the advice you receive.

Email Marketing
for Complex Sales Cycles

Chapter 1

Email Marketing... Relatively Easy, and Extremely Powerful—When You Do it Right

Email generated a lot of excitement among marketing executives when it first came along.

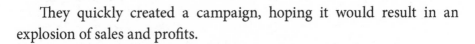

They saw the potential: a cheap, easy way to reach a huge number of prospects.

Some jumped in with enthusiasm.

They quickly created a campaign, hoping it would result in an explosion of sales and profits.

But the bomb never went off, so they concluded that email marketing was a dud.

In actuality, all they did was light a fuse.

They never built the explosive device to attach to it.

Here's what they probably did.

They bought an email list and sent out an ad.

They waited, but nothing happened.

So they bought another list sent out another ad.

They were sued for spamming even though they could prove they weren't.

At that point they decided, "Hey, this is more trouble than it's worth."

And they gave up.

Mindset matters — you've been brainwashed to do something different

It's essential to understand how email marketing works and embrace the truth that it's different from time-honored and commonly accepted marketing techniques.

Failure to understand this new thinking can — almost certainly will — result in failure and frustration.

When you examine what it takes to do an email campaign properly, you might recoil in horror at first.

You have to have the software and hardware to make it work, which might mean making a significant capital investment.

It requires a shift in thinking by management, which can sometimes be perilous.

It means retraining sales and support staff, which is bound to meet with resistance.

And even when you have everything in place, you'll be tempted to think you're not getting anywhere — especially if you're still expecting that "explosion" of sales and profits.

The people who succeed — and profit — do it because they iron out a few initial wrinkles. They learn from their mistakes. Soon they're able to deploy an incredibly efficient system that attracts huge numbers of prospects.

And they're the kind of prospects everybody wants: narrowly targeted, intensely focused — and ready to buy.

But it doesn't happen the first time you send out an email, even if you send it out to a huge number of prospects.

It's like climbing a hill. You do it a step at a time, and you may even slip and scrape a knee along the way.

But once you reach the top, you can set a snowball in motion down the other side.

You get a rolling, ever-growing mass that gathers prospects as it moves forward.

And once it reaches speed, it rumbles very quickly through your marketplace, sustained by its own momentum.

That's when the benefits pile up: low maintenance, low risk, low cost — and high profit.

Chapter 2

Change Your Mindset, Change Your Future

Before you can learn to do an email marketing program, you have to unlearn, or at least modify, some assumptions you may have about using the Internet and email to help you sell.

 To market effectively and profitably, you'll have to do a lot more than build a website and wait for orders to start rolling in.

You'll have to understand that you can't just rely on search engines to help people find you.

You'll have to accept that vehicles you've used for years to generate leads for your sales staff—trade shows, brochures, advertising spreads, commercials on radio and TV—will need to be de-emphasized, possibly even abandoned, because of new avenues opened up by the Internet.

Email marketing will require a change of perspective, especially in organizations where people like to keep doing things "the way we've always done them," or would be tempted to say, "If it ain't broke, why fix it?"

To use an analogy of the computer age, you'll have to "hit the restart button" on your mindset.

Email is very much like the telephone when that first came along. New technology that took "some getting used to."

Most people didn't understand how it worked. Fewer foresaw its potential.

But can you imagine anyone surviving in business *without* the telephone in the last hundred years?

Email and the Internet will surpass the telephone as the information vehicle of choice in the next few years.

 In that time — sooner for some — you will either have a comprehensive email component to your marketing and your customer service, or your business will fail. It will be as critical as somebody saying, "Well, we have a great business but we don't take phone calls." It just won't be acceptable.

In fact, it will be suicidal.

But just having email as an everyday communication tool won't be enough.

You'll have to use it to find prospects, befriend them, educate them, and finally — sell them.

That's what this book is about.

Will you be able to "delete" the sales staff?

Am I saying that email marketing will replace your sales force?

Am I saying that you can send one email and immediately separate yourself from the dozens — or hundreds — of other emails that land in your prospect's inbox almost any day?

Am I saying that someone will buy a $2,000, or a $50,000, or a $500,000 product or service because they received an email from you saying "Please purchase this?"

Not at all.

Email marketing means you have a system and a process. It's not just a single event.

Think of the Super Bowl as an analogy. The winner sits atop the world of pro football. But to reach that point, it took five weeks of training camp, sixteen regular season games, a series of playoff games, and then finally a win in the big game itself.

That's the way it is with an email marketing plan. Certain steps have to be followed, and certain elements implemented, to ensure success. Each step, each element, represents a progression in the process. Each step, each element, successfully executed, brings you closer to your ultimate goal.

In the NFL, it's pre-season, regular season, and post-season.

In an email marketing plan, it's the process of persuasion, the process of conversion, and the process of closing.

The process of persuasion

Before you can sell anything to anyone, you need to find people who want to buy. With email, you can often do so comprehensively and inexpensively.

You start by sending out something to a massive number of prospects (with their permission, of course — more on that later).

With that first email, you just want them to raise a hand indicating they might be interested. That's where the process of persuasion through an email marketing system really begins.

As with direct marketing, you're hoping 1% or 2% or even 3% will respond.

Here's where most companies start getting excited as responses pile up in their mailboxes.

And here's where most companies make their first — and frequently their fatal — mistake.

The process of conversion

When your typical sales pro opens his or her inbox after a mass mail-out, the first reaction is glee.

They're likely to raise both arms in the air and shout "yes," thinking they have a lock on a new Jaguar, a house in the Hamptons, or debt-free Ivy League educations for their kids.

They don't realize at first that these leads are fundamentally different than the leads that may be coming in through traditional sales channels.

Converting leads like those into sales requires retraining your brain.

But here's the good news.

Once you have a group of interested people, it's pretty easy to engineer that conversion through a persuasively designed email marketing system.

Now here's the bad news.

The whole thing can run off in the ditch if you don't do it right.

There are seven major mistakes you can make along the way that will cause the process to collapse. I'll tell you more about those later.

The process of closing

The third and final element of the email marketing process actually has very little to do with email.

It's the process of closing. And here's where your sales staff goes to work doing what it does best. This is the stage where face-to-face meetings take place, a proposal is created and, hopefully, someone signs on a dotted line and takes out their checkbook.

In other words, an email marketing process is designed to "get you invited to the party."

Where you go from there depends on the talent and skill of your sales pros.

And here's why your sales pros will eventually come to love what an email marketing system will do for them.

If you're currently converting one of every twenty-five leads into a sale, you can probably improve that number significantly thanks to email.

That's because the process is so automatic, systematic and repeatable.

You can blanket a huge number of prospects at the beginning, and with each successive step, separate them into groups like "not interested," "mildly interested," "very interested," or "feverishly interested."

Your sales people focus first on those who seem to be very interested or feverishly interested.

Your lead-to-sale ratio improves to fifteen-to-one or even ten-to-one.

And you do it at an extremely low cost.

More sales at less expense.

Isn't that what we're all shooting for?

How to accelerate the process

The worst thing about email marketing is this: you find out very quickly when you've failed.

The best thing about email marketing is this: you find out very quickly when you've succeeded.

Most important of all to your bottom line is this: it can all happen automatically and systematically, and the results are quickly and irrefutably verifiable.

And it all starts with a simple click of a mouse — once you've designed the system, of course.

Because of the automation email marketing offers, you can measure the results in not weeks, but days... and you get an early indication within hours.

Your ability to move your sales process forward quickly, flexibly, fluidly — and inexpensively — is unsurpassed.

And that's a huge benefit when your sales process tends to be long and complex.

Chapter 3

Six Special Needs of Complex Sales Cycles

There are a growing number of books written about selling on the Internet.

Sadly, if you struggle with a complex sales cycle, much of the advice is irrelevant.

The materials are directed at the following scenario: A visitor finds a website through a search engine or some other means, reads the page, and within minutes, decides whether to buy or not.

If you have a complex sales cycle that takes place over weeks, months, or years, you'll find few sources of marketing advice.

That's important because things that work in shorter sales cycles sometimes work against you in a long one.

White becomes black and black becomes white.

For example, you get excellent results in a one-page website if you can convey a sense of urgency or scarcity to the prospect.

But you'll be taking a large cannon and aiming it at your head if you do that in a complex situation where it would be perceived as "pressure."

You don't shoot for fast dollars with an email marketing system.

And your mindset has to reflect that fact.

But patience pays. And it pays in a number of important ways.

Dramatically increase your sales revenue

There's no doubt that you have to absorb some expenses during the development stage of an email marketing program.

There's a lot of time, energy, and money invested before a payoff takes place.

But once you make that investment, create the campaign, and launch it, the returns flow in predictably, reliably, frequently — and if you do things right — formidably.

Done well, it can produce a huge and positive impact on your balance sheet. This is especially true considering most complex sales cycles involve expensive "big ticket" products.

Suppose, for instance, you're selling a $75,000 product, and you typically sell three a quarter. If an email marketing system can help you add one more without an additional investment of time or money, you'd be adding 33% to your revenue that quarter.

Numbers like that would make you a hero on Wall Street.

Reduce the laborious, tedious, and humiliating process of getting sales started

Ask a professional sales person, "What are your worst nightmares?" and you'll probably get answers like these:

- "I start a new job and on my first day my sales manager hands me the Yellow Pages and says, 'Start making calls…'"
- "I'm assigned a new territory and when I mention it to someone at the company Christmas party, they say, 'Oh… So you're the one who drew the short straw…'"
- "As I'm making initial calls to introduce myself to prospects in a new territory, one says to me, 'Doesn't Joe Schmoe work for your company? I'll never buy anything from the company Joe Schmoe works for.'"

With an email marketing system, those things don't happen.

Substantially reduce your costs

How would you like to reduce the time your top sales pros spend on trivial administrative activities?

If they could fill their schedules with appointments in front of bona fide, pre-qualified prospects, couldn't they make more sales?

That's what an email marketing system does for you.

It eliminates guesswork. It filters out "tire kickers."

It saves you money by reducing the time-and-money wasting "fishing expeditions" your sales people make trying to find prospects that are ready to buy.

You always hear sales people say things like, "It's a numbers game. A hundred calls will result in ten appointments. Ten appointments will result in three proposals. Three proposals will result in one sale…"

The "numbers game" argument falls apart when you have an effective email marketing system.

You eliminate those ninety calls where your sales person has to talk their way past a gatekeeper or leave a message on voice mail — three or four times — and they wind up not getting an appointment out of it anyway.

Email marketing also reduces phone expenses, travel expenses, and a host of other money-wasters usually associated with trying to make the "numbers game" work.

Remove the uncertainty about meeting your sales objectives month-in and month-out

With a well-constructed email marketing system, you're constantly and continuously "sweeping the marketplace," automatically locating any activity that may be of interest.

You're drawing out most — if not all — of the quality leads that are available.

You'll also begin to grow a backlog of activity because you're reaching out to people when their minds are open and receptive, rather than when they've already made up their mind about a purchase decision.

The more you can focus on prospects that are ready to buy, the easier it is to hit quotas and forecasts.

Make sure a competitor isn't tapping a part of the market you're not reaching

How often have you heard someone say, "We have a lock on that segment of the market?"

In fact, companies who make that claim are already working off their existing contact list.

They may not be aware of a new person just coming into the market, or a new person who has just been promoted from a different division in the company. But those people will generally show up on a good mailing list.

So when someone claims, "We're really wired into that marketplace. We know everything that's going on," an email marketing system is a great way to find out if that's true.

Very often they discover it's not anywhere near as "true" as they thought.

They're astounded at the number of opportunities they're overlooking or deals they're missing.

Once they spot openings they didn't realize were there, they can take action before competitors start to move in.

Accelerate the speed at which deals move through your sales process

Email marketing allows your sales people more time to be on the phone or in the office with prospects.

The less your sales pros have to fight paper dragons or waste time on other low-return activities, the less likely sales will "escape" or not materialize as expected.

They can stay in touch more frequently with top prospects. As more time passes between contacts, chances increase that prospects will develop misperceptions about your company or products.

By reducing the amount of time your high-performance, relationship-oriented sales people spend "fishing," you increase the amount of time they spend solving their prospects' problems. That means they have more time to respond quickly to their prospects' needs.

Email marketing gives your competition less of an opening to grow a relationship with your prospect, or even steal business away from you.

Chapter 4

The Disappointment of Email Marketing

Four typical ways executives go wrong— and nine excuses they make

Martin had just attended a regional seminar for CEOs.

 It was an opportunity to "sharpen the sword," gain insight into his business, reflect on his past efforts and calculate his strategy for his next big growth push.

He attended a seminar about using email for lead generation.

Interesting...

The speaker promised that a well-crafted program could provide a continuous flow of leads while lowering his sales cost.

Boy, this really had an appeal! His sales people were always complaining about the awful leads they brought back from their trade shows, and how they had to scratch and claw their way into deals!

He took notes, understood the general idea, and on the way back home crafted a plan to make email a valuable part of his sales arsenal.

Fast-forward 4 months.

Martin is sitting at his desk, looking at the results of his campaign. He's shaking his head.

No orders and, in fact, no really viable leads.

And in the way that CEOs sometimes do, he concludes that his business was just not a good fit for email marketing.

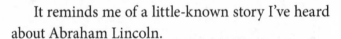

I call this "jumping to the wrong conclusion," even when the facts seem to support your analysis.

It reminds me of a little-known story I've heard about Abraham Lincoln.

Before he began his political career, Lincoln was representing a client in a trial in Illinois. He wanted the jury to understand that you can have your facts straight and still draw the wrong conclusion from them.

Here's the story he told:

A 6-year-old boy came running into the farmhouse from the barn, breathless.

"Ma," he shouted. "Sister Sue is up in the hayloft with neighbor John. She's a-liftin' up her dress. He's a-pullin' down his pants. You better get out there right away before they pee all over the hay!"

The moral of the story: you can have your facts straight, but…

Let's look at some of the ways well-intentioned marketers can jump to the wrong conclusion.

Confusing the beginning of a sales cycle with the end of it

I recently spoke to a retail chain owner who told me, "We collected email addresses in our shops for months. Then one day we sent out a special offer on some equipment. We didn't make a single sale."

 You'll hear similar stories from other people, and you almost always find out that their email marketing "campaign" wasn't a campaign at all.

It was more like a shot in the dark.

A single email sent out to a list (even if it's a list of your own club members) has a low likelihood of success.

Email works best when it's used to begin a sales cycle, not finish it. In other words, email is a door opener. An introduction. An offer to get to know each other and become friends.

It's like asking someone out on a date. You don't propose marriage at the end of the first one.

And you'll probably be disappointed if you try.

Leave the real romancing to the people who are good at it — your sales pros.

Sending out spam

I spent several pages examining the spam issue at the beginning of this book. But some of the key points deserve re-emphasis.

If you email a list of people without their explicit permission, you are guilty of spamming.

If your list comes from a third party, your offer must be relevant to the relationship the third party has to it. So avoid the friend that says, "Hey, I have this great list or this association" or that kind of thing.

 It's spam because you don't have permission to contact that person, and that creates a bunch of problems for you.

For starters, you can have your email service shut down by your Internet service provider.

You can even be sued.

There is a growing number of cases in which vendors who broadcast emails to a large number of people have been hit with large judgments.

State and local governments are working hard to stem the onslaught of spam and rushing regulations into law. As with any new legislation there are plenty of unforeseen and unintended consequences, and even a well intentioned emailer can unknowingly run afoul of new legislation.

So be careful. It's a fluid, changing area of the law.

Make sure you know what's legal and what isn't before you hit the "Send" key.

That said as I write this, there are some generally accepted precautions you can take to protect yourself.

Every email has to have some source of referral. The recipient has to be able to figure out why it's there. Something like:

"You're receiving this email because you're a subscriber to the Financial Times newsletter. And when you subscribed you said you'd be interested in receiving information from third parties."

Without such an explanation, you'll get bombarded with hostile email or "flames," and you'll be reported as a spammer. And if you use your domain name in your email, your service provider could shut down your whole email system.

So you really want to be careful to put an explanation of how you obtained their address in plain sight.

Second, your offer has to have some connection to the original reason people signed up for that list.

If they're looking for health information, it's okay to talk to them about vitamins or even Viagra.

But don't ask them to buy a lawnmower or refinance their mortgage.

Third, you have to give them a way to get off the list, or "unsubscribe." This is also called "opting out."

Doing these three things will eliminate the vast majority of the problems that you would have sending your message out to a large number of people who don't know you.

It won't eliminate resentment completely, however.

In a list of several thousand people there are bound to be a few who are having a bad day and want to take out their frustrations on someone.

Expect some flames.

 You can usually spot them right away because they hit your inbox in a string of capitalized four-letter words.

Flames happen. Make sure you remove the senders from your list, don't take it personally, and whatever you do, don't respond with some four-letter words of your own.

Just move on.

Falling victim to a "list scam"

One fast and easy way to waste plenty of money — and get a lot of flames or possibly even lawsuits — is to fall for a scam that preys upon the entrepreneur eager to "dive in" to email marketing.

They'll tell you, "We can find any list you want," and they'll offer to sell one to you.

Watch out.

Brokers who have good permission-based mailing lists usually rent them. They're too valuable to sell.

A friend of mine who wishes to remain anonymous (you'll understand why in a moment) recently thought he was getting a bargain when he bought a list of 50,000 names for $15,000.

He wrote up an email singing the praises of his $22,000 product and blasted it out.

He didn't make a single sale even though it was a recognizable product with an excellent reputation in the industry.

The list, in fact, seemed to be a random collection of names pulled off websites and news groups on the Internet — a sure recipe for failure.

Failing before even trying

 Email systems don't work for some people because they never give the system a chance. People make assumptions about their market, their processes, their prospects, and their company's image that defeat them before they even get in the game.

Below are the nine most frequent reasons I hear from people who say they don't want to execute an email marketing program.

"It's 'beneath' us"

Some companies feel uncomfortable renting a list and emailing a prospect "cold."

They say, "Oh gee, isn't that kind of smarmy or kind of ahhhh, you know, distasteful? We really don't feel comfortable just casting out our marketing message like that."

You have to realize that when people sign up for a good opt-in list, it's usually because they have an ongoing interest in an area or a problem.

They'll glance over all those spam emails they get if you can persuade them there's some possibility you'll actually help educate them or solve that problem.

There's an old story about the one kid who gets a horse for Christmas, and another kid who gets a room full of horse manure. The kid with the room full of horse manure keeps shoveling through it like crazy because he's convinced there has to be a horse in there somewhere.

If you really want that horse, you'll sometimes have to shovel through some manure trying to find it.

And someone who has a problem will scan past all the "Viagra" and "Refinance Now!" emails to open one that they even slightly suspect is useful.

That's where your persuasion approach becomes critical.

Your persuasion approach tempts the reader to turn off a "filter."

You just need to connect with them enough so that they'll click the mouse and open the email.

Once your prospect crosses that threshold they're much more susceptible to persuasion because you know that they've already flipped the switch and turned off their filtering system. They've "raised their hand" to signal that they're serious about finding a solution to their problem.

You find those people when you get a good list. Trade show attendees, magazine subscribers, and book buyers fall into this category.

And usually, to get lists like that, you have to rent them.

I'll talk more about persuasion approach in Chapter 11.

"Our sales process is too complicated"

An email marketing system actually works beautifully with complex sales processes.

The system forces you to break down your cycle into basic elements. In doing so, you can often spot multiple entry points in your pool of prospects.

It can be devastatingly effective because you can blanket your entire prospect population every time you send out a message. If you're overlooking any opportunities or new "entry points," you'll be able to spot them.

"We depend on relationships and face-to-face contact"

If you think email won't work for you because your sales process requires personal contact, think again.

With email marketing, your prospects get to see your sales staff more often, not less.

Recent surveys have reported that sales people only spend about 15% of their time in front of prospects, face-to-face.

Furthermore, the percentage has been declining for the last few years.

Given that, you'd certainly want them in front of the best prospects wouldn't you?

And guess what?

Because email handles a lot of the routine preliminary administrative chores normally handled by your sales person, he or she gets to spend time with more of the best prospects.

That makes for better relationships.

It also makes for more sales.

"Our marketing department generates all our leads"

In some companies, this is actually true. But my experience tells me that more often than not, leads produced in traditional ways by the marketing department are of lower quality and offer less potential than leads generated by an email system.

Think back over the last quarter. How many of your sales resulted from leads that were generated by typical marketing department tactics: trade shows, brochures, advertising, etc.?

If the answer is "not many," then an email system is probably a good idea — if not an absolute necessity.

"Our market is so small we can't use mass methods"

Yes, email marketing campaigns work superbly in markets with thousands or even hundreds of thousands of prospects. But I know of cases where they've been effective when the prospect base was only a few hundred.

It may be even more important if you serve a smaller niche because the company that communicates well to that audience will garner a larger slice of the potential business from them.

"Our prospects are too sophisticated"

People read their email, even if they say they don't. Many even open spam emails. The spam industry would be collapsing if it wasn't paying off.

It's kind of like the National Enquirer.

How many people that you know actually admit to reading it?

But they continue to sell more newspapers than any other publication in the United States.

Email is the same way.

People will say they hate spam, but if they're desperately trying to find a solution to a problem, and they see something in a subject line that gives them hope — they'll open it.

You're not spamming, of course. You're getting names legitimately from a reputable list broker or some other permission-based source.

But you probably get the idea.

And here's something else to consider.

How many people that you know had an email address ten years ago? Probably less that one in a hundred.

How many people that you know don't have an email address today?

In fact, one client, who initially rejected the thought of using email in his business, now checks his email even after a trip to the bathroom in the middle of the night.

Email has become a fixture in our lives, and it's not going to go away anytime soon.

Conversely as the spammers of the world are ferreted out and shut down by regulation and spam-filtering, legitimate permission-based email will improve its effectiveness as a medium.

No matter how sophisticated your prospects are, they'll open an email if they think it might help them.

"We're just a little company in a big pond"

If this is the case, you really need an email marketing system.

You probably can't afford to compete with the big companies by dropping lots of dollars into mass advertising. That gets expensive.

Yet you still need to differentiate yourself enough to carve out a niche and get a share of the market.

Email allows you to do that for a lot less cash than it costs to run a commercial during the Super Bowl or a full page ad in an industry publication.

"We can't afford it"

As the saying goes, "You can't afford not to!"

Think about all the time your high-performance sales people spend doing things that email could be doing for them.

Add up the hours and multiply that by their hourly rate.

You pay pennies for email to handle most of those same tasks.

When you run the numbers, you'll find that even though you'll spend $15,000 – $35,000 to launch your email system, you'll recoup that investment in a relatively short time.

You've heard the phrase, "Just add water," haven't you?

Think of your email marketing system in similar terms. Once it's set up and operating, all you have to do is "add water" — permission-based names.

What most entrepreneurs fail to realize is that companies can use the same basic email marketing system, with very little maintenance or modification, for as long as two to three years.

You really have to look at amortizing your original investment over the span of years you plan to use the program.

In the meantime, the system saves you many times that amount by relieving your staff of some of the mindless, low-productivity tasks they'd have to perform without it.

It can be expensive, especially when you're renting good lists. Expect to pay from 25 to 55 cents per name!

But here's something else to consider.

Even though you rent a list in the beginning, you begin to build your own in-house database as people respond to your offerings. Once you have those names, they're yours—and from then on, your emails to them are virtually free.

In some cases, you might even reach the point where you no longer have to rent lists from brokers, and cash is coming in as the system runs itself.

"Our staff isn't smart enough to figure this out—it's too complicated"

I hear this one a lot.

If this is the case in your company, then you're a perfect candidate for a turnkey system.

Relying on a trained outside consultant to get your team up and running allows you to skip over the sometimes painful problems of getting your system developed and running on its own.

And in my experience, you will probably spend about half as much as you ultimately would by doing it yourself… unless of course you have the expertise on staff.

That said, if members of your staff use email today, they can manage a well crafted lead generation system with a small amount of training.

Summary

I've just mentioned a few faulty assumptions people tend to make about email marketing.

Once you discard them and accept email as a valid marketing vehicle, there are still some commonly held myths that need debunking to move you on your way to profitability.

I'll cover those in the next chapter.

Chapter 5
Critical Mindset Shifts

"Myth-information" in the marketplace

 Several years ago, some "hot dots"—i.e. suddenly over-capitalized dotcom companies —strutted their stuff by showing off during commercial breaks of the NFL's annual championship extravaganza.

These companies made a Super Bowl-sized splash on the small screen.

And then they made a equally big flash in the proverbial pan.

Their stories typify the sad truth about the "dotcom" boom—and the "dotbomb" bust that followed.

The dotcom boomers preached "Build it and they will come…"

In other words, put a website out there in cyberspace and people will punch credit card numbers into it by the millions.

Those dreams evaporated—along with about seven trillion dollars on Wall Street—in 2000 to 2001.

Those who survived learned the truth about using the Internet to market. They discarded the myths and developed certain mindsets — "givens," if you will.

But the average business person who doesn't follow every twist and turn of the technology market may still have some contaminated thinking in this area.

What was conventional wisdom a few short years ago has been unmasked.

I'll show its true face in this chapter.

Company websites don't sell

Successful marketers have begun to realize that the traditional company website is little better than a Yellow Pages ad.

A lot of companies have invested significantly in their websites, dumping six or even seven figures into their web presence.

Some of these sites look fabulous and even attract lots of visitors. Everyone in the company points to them with pride.

Everyone that is, except the sales people.

The sales people become the first to figure out that pretty pictures don't necessarily produce prospects.

They learn quickly that a website alone won't generate leads to help them meet their quotas.

Research shows, in fact, that many websites actually frustrate prospects that want to buy.

Visitors get lost in the navigation and can't find information they want.

They get irritated because they feel they don't have control.

Most sites celebrate the company's products and services, crow about their tradition, show pictures of senior management and list their degrees and the schools they graduated from.

All in all, many company websites succeed fabulously at congratulating themselves.

But they never talk about how they can help solve their visitors' problems.

And that's why they fail.

Every lead generated must be followed through

Do you treat your prospects like grunions?

In California, several times a year an amazing thing happens — grunions procreate!

The grunion is a fish that comes up on the shore with the tide on a full moon. The female burrows into the soft sand and lays her eggs. Then the male comes up and fertilizes those eggs.

It is a great spectacle for parents and kids. It's always late at night, on a full moon. Parents take the kids to the beach and watch this unfold with great excitement and anticipation.

A single wave crashes onto the beach and suddenly the whole beach is covered with grunions, twitching and jumping and doing all the things fish do when they spawn. (Kind of like your favorite industry trade show!) It's a fabulous sight and, as you can imagine, there's a lot of excitement.

Hundreds of people turn out. They roll up their pants and everybody gets wet and sandy picking up slippery fish.

In California, it's the only fish you don't need a license to catch.

In an instant, another wave rolls in, scoops up the thousands of grunions and the beach is quiet, as if nothing ever happened.

Tired, cold and wet, all the participants filter back to their cars with kids and plastic bags of fish in tow.

You may have seen a program on one of the nature channels about this phenomenon.

Toward the end of the show, the commentator asked an expert from the Scripps Oceanographic Institute, "And what do people do with the grunions that they catch?"

He responds, "Usually they take them home in a plastic bag, put them in their freezer and throw them out in about 2 to 3 years."

Unfortunately, that's exactly what most companies do with their leads after a trade show!

They take them back to the office, gloat over how many they caught, and then the file spins around on their disk untouched for the next 3 years.

After the excitement of that fresh crop of new leads from a trade show or lead generation campaign, the leads all go into hiding.

Some marketing literature I've read suggested that as many as 80% of the leads gathered at trade shows are never contacted after the show is over.

Most companies have been doing business that way for such a long time that they accept such neglect as a given. Their mindset is, "We found the leads; it's somebody else's job to turn them into orders."

Email technology dramatically changes the rules because it can be programmed to consistently, aggressively, even belligerently follow up once a lead enters the system.

Every lead is pursued, every opportunity explored — automatically and systematically — until the prospect either buys… or "opts out."

In other words, "the fortune is in the follow-up." And most companies don't do enough of it.

The Triangle of Hidden Opportunity

Let's talk a little bit more about grunions. And geometry.

Imagine a triangle, divided into four layers.

At the very top of the triangle you see "Ready Buyers." These are people who have their checkbooks out and are ready to pay you.

Just below the top of the triangle, there are the folks who will be buying soon.

Below them, in the third tier, are people who will buy someday.

At the base of the triangle are those who will never buy at all.

Everyone wants to work with the people at the top of the triangle, of course, because the cash register is ready to ring.

But there are 3 reasons that the people at the top of the triangle may not be your best prospects:

1. Their buying criteria has probably been influenced heavily by your competitors if they are that far along.

2. They are the easiest to identify through traditional marketing methods and all your competitors are piling in trying to grab the deal.
3. In the face of all that competition, price-cutting is frequently merciless. You'll spend a lot of money to get the deal and have little margin at the end.

An email marketing campaign reduces or even eliminates those negatives.

Email empowers you to move those who are lower on the triangle toward the top through automated, targeted releases of information that predispose them to buy from you — and only you.

Prospects buy on their timetable — not yours

Noted marketing genius Jay Abraham likes to say "life is a moving parade."

Your prospects are moving through cycles of continuous, sometimes even tumultuous change.

And they do things on their timetable, not yours.

They don't care about your forecasts or quotas. They don't care that you're coming up on the end of a quarter and you're below your goals. They're not necessarily ready to buy when you're ready to sell.

Think of all the things that compete for their attention.

They may have just changed jobs. Maybe they had a bad quarter and there's a cap on spending. Maybe there are unsettling changes in their industry.

So even if they've expressed interest in your offering at some point, you're not going to hit them at the moment that they move into the top of the triangle and are ready to buy — unless you've already doing a regular sequence of contact and follow-up.

The secret to getting the best performance out of your sales staff

Today, sales managers everywhere are frustrated by the under-utilization of their sales force.

Companies with five, ten, twenty or more people who are dedicated to selling are especially susceptible.

These people are often spend time and energy working in the lower sections of the triangle. They're dragging in marginal clients — really — "suspects" instead of "prospects."

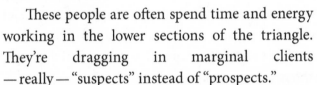

To unqualified "suspects" the value of solving the problem at hand is not that great. The unfortunate impact is that your sales people have to expend more energy turning half-hearted "suspects" into sales.

Sadly, many of them clog up your funnel. In complex or high technology sales processes, a face-to-face sales call typically runs about $2,000. You might burn through seven to ten meetings before you actually get a prospect to say "Yes."

Of course, there's a possible downside. You might make four to six sales calls and then get a "No!" or even something more dissatisfying: "Well, we decided not to do anything about that right now."

A well conceived, systematic email program keeps your sales staff focused on the legitimate prospects at the top of the triangle. You can minimize the under-utilization of a multi-person sales force.

Here's something else an email program will do for your sales team: keep their morale — and their production — high.

When customers are moving at their own pace, and your sales people are falling short of their quotas, sales managers often start applying pressure to get the numbers in line. "Get 'out there' and talk to more people," sales people are told.

Of course, this frustrates the sales people. Because of circumstances beyond their control, there may not be many prospects "out there" ready to buy.

Email marketing relieves some of the pressure by managing the prospect pipeline to assure a flow of good prospects. Sales people don't have to hurry prospects along, trying to close them prematurely — because they can better control the rate at which people come into the top of the funnel.

Sales people love it because they get to do what they like best. Help their clients, grow their relationships, close sales — and make quotas.

"Oh Lord, please give me just one more dotcom boom..."

The sales executive who thinks that another boom cycle will cure all ills just doesn't understand the problem.

You might be thinking, "Well, it's just a tough economic climate right now.

"It's difficult out there. The last few years have seen the worst economy any of us have seen in our working lives.

"The dotcom bubble burst... there's terrorism... war... more competition chasing fewer dollars.

"But it's turning around and I'll be on Easy Street — if I can just scramble around and get enough deals going — even if they are a little far a-field from my core business."

This is the common approach to a weak economy.

In my experience, this could be limiting to your career at a minimum, or worse — damaging to your company.

As more and more companies reach beyond their core products or services, seeking additional revenue streams, their margins shrink and the amount of time it takes to close a sale grows by leaps and bounds.

You'll face a bigger challenge determining where there's a good fit for your product or service, so you have to be more sophisticated developing that book of business.

Email marketing programs help you zero in.

You can determine more quickly — and inexpensively — where your offering fits your prospect like the proverbial glove.

In only pursuing business that is a good fit, you disqualify the most damaging and unlikely prospects before you spend much money on them.

And when you move to that posture, you can decide where to utilize your sales force more efficiently and profitably.

In the end, pursuing "good fit" business will give you a healthier company. The problem has always been finding enough of it to make your numbers. Using the lever of email you now have the tool to get that done.

Chapter 6

Three Critical Stages of Success

The irrational exuberance of the dotcom boom produced a crop of sales managers and sales tactics that persist to this day — many of them at best ineffective, and at worst destructive.

In my work with clients I find a simple ferreting out of some of these unproductive strategies results in significant, immediate improvement in the way the sales organization works.

The first step in that process is getting executives to understand that there are 3 distinct segments to the sales cycle. In each of those segments you apply different strategies and tactics. What makes sense in the first segment maybe counter-productive by the third segment.

In the rest of this chapter, I'm going to look at three parts of the sales cycle most involved with getting deals done. They are: finding opportunities, moving deals forward, and bringing deals home.

Finding opportunities

If you make a $50,000 product you're probably not going sell a lot of them — especially with a one-shot email (although rarely does a week go by that I don't see somebody trying to pull this one off).

But with that same effort, using an email crafted to open a sale (rather than close it) you have a realistic possibility of adding legitimate, qualified prospects who need your solution to your forecast.

And more important to your bottom line, you can build rapport, educate and engender appreciation systematically — before you ever send your sales people out on those $2,000 face-to-face meetings.

 Under the old marketing model — which companies thrash themselves with daily — your sales team would grab that shy information-seeker by the lapels and shake them until they either bought, threw you out, or died.

They would engage the prospect, qualify them, build rapport, educate them, grow the relationship, assess problems, identify solutions, and — finally — make the sale.

What most sales execs don't realize (and this may be the most important concept in this entire book) is that by effectively using email, you can systematize and automate a lot of the pre-close engagement activity.

That frees up your sales rep for the very valuable, very expensive face-to-face or voice-to-ear contact at a time when the prospect is most receptive.

Moving deals forward

As you move to the next segment of the cycle, it's very important to stay focused on problems that are most troubling to your prospect.

During this segment you have the opportunity to use the power of automated systems to feed your prospect a customized stream of information that helps them further qualify themselves either in (or out) of your sales funnel.

During this segment, it's a mistake to start selling the product too aggressively (entrepreneurs struggle with this concept). You'll have to fight the temptation to sing your product's praises, claiming you have the best widget in the tri-state area, or that you guarantee service for eternity.

You want to stay away from any sort of "selling" in this part of your email process.

Your goal is to convince your prospect that you are somebody who can help them solve their problems, instead of someone who gets invited in, shows up and says, "Well, here's the brochure and here's the price list and we have 10% off if you order by Friday. Sign here."

Bringing deals home

This is where your highly trained, relationship oriented sales people do their best work.

They enter this stage of the process with the email system having sorted the wheat from the chaff and, ever so subtly, philosophically aligned your prospect with your intended solution.

This part of the cycle is really beyond the scope of this book and more appropriately addressed by my able colleagues in the sales training field.

Chapter 7
Unhooking — The Process of Un-Training Your Brain

The process of destroying your faulty assumptions about the use of email marketing in the sales process is so critical that I'm going to tell some things that fly in the face of conventional marketing wisdom. You'll have to discard some tenets that have gained credence through the years.

I call this process "unhooking," or "un-training your brain."

Stop prospecting with expensive sales people

In companies with complex or multi-phase sales processes, the salespeople spend a lot of time in "engagement activities." They collect dozens or even hundreds of leads and start "dialing for dollars."

After whittling them down, they spend more time meeting with them in person.

After that, they spend even more time creating and presenting proposals, then finally closing the sale.

The final stages are where good sales people shine. They excel at relationship skills, they're very good at bonding, listening, and understanding.

Does it make sense to take that high performance sales person and sit them down for hours of "smiling and dialing?" Do you really want your "stars" making dozens of calls only to connect with a few people? After an endless barrage of voicemails, gatekeepers, and busy signals, they're bound to get frustrated and burned out.

The promise of an effective email marketing system is that it eliminates (or substantially reduces) the first cycle, and "tees" your sales team up to operate in cycles two and three, free of the weariness of "scratch and claw" dialing.

Once fully tuned, the promise of the email marketing system is that you get invited into a sale because of your expertise, rather than "injected" due to your persistence.

The injection approach also can create in its wake a significant amount of animosity and irritation.

A good email system automates the first cycle of the process and maybe even part of the second — finding opportunities and moving deals along. So your sales people can concentrate on the things they do best, which are also the things that make everyone the most money.

Forget the "decision-maker"

Traditional sales training has always preached the importance of "finding the decision-maker."

"Boy," you'd hear someone say, "if we can just get to the CFO or the vice president of purchasing or the vice president of IT or the head of operations or whatever, we're going to get this deal."

Some companies even paid a bonus just for booking a meeting with the person who actually made the final call.

In the new marketing reality, this concept crumbles.

As our economy labors under threats of terrorism, financial weakness, and technology upheavals, many companies have downsized, responsibilities have changed, and organizational charts have been redrawn.

Senior managers often find themselves dealing with a much greater span of control and an increased number of direct reports.

They wind up spending more time in crisis mode, stomping out fires rather than visualizing and planning future directions. They're getting interrupted more often.

So the decision-maker is no longer the person who can sit down and thoughtfully evaluate your proposal.

Consequently, a strategy targeting that particular individual doesn't work as well as it used to.

In fact, in the new marketing model, you forget the decision-maker.

You look instead for the person who has the greatest direct responsibility for solving the problem your product or service will solve.

Email is a perfect "force multiplier." To use a fishing analogy, it allows you to "throw a lot of lines in the water" simultaneously and hook the attention of the right person — someone you can develop into an advocate for your version of the solution.

Abandon unproductive legacy marketing

Near the end of the 1990's, trade shows became an extremely popular lead generation vehicle.

Your sales team returned from Atlanta or Anaheim or Las Vegas with a fishbowl full of business cards or entry forms. They hit the phones doing follow-up.

You collected trade show leads in batches — sometimes they were very large batches, but they were batches nonetheless. And you might go months, or even an entire year before you saw another batch.

Worst of all, a lot of those cards in the fish bowl didn't turn out to be productive leads.

Trade shows are still around, but many companies have lost enthusiasm for them.

They require a big commitment of time and money and while they accomplish a number of good and necessary things, they are not the most efficient way to produce sales.

Contrast them with an email lead generation system, on the other hand, which costs almost nothing once it's in place.

And, more important, it produces a continues flow of reliable leads, running on its own, all day, all night, all week, all month, all year.

When you set it up right, it gets your sales force invited in — instead of them having to fight their way in, competing with a bunch of other salespeople the client is too busy to see.

 There's one more important benefit.

By the time you're invited in, you've already established your credibility and expertise before the meeting.

And the same goes for...

Large advertising spreads... newsletters... glossy brochures... seminars and road shows.

Many companies do some or all of these things trying to generate leads.

Here's the downside to those media: they all tend to look alike.

For example, Microsoft is the big daddy of the software market and is very conspicuous in all the business and trade media. Their advertising borders on trendy and esoteric and it lacks edge — but it looks great!

Sadly, many fledgling software companies do their best to mimic Microsoft (monkey see, monkey do).

Face it. You're never going to "out-Microsoft" Microsoft. You are only setting yourself up for failure.

And once your prospects go beyond image and into substance, they'll realize that you're not Microsoft or IBM (or whoever the leader is in your industry).

Some image-conscious executives, impressed by your artsy ad, will quickly blow you off their short list when they realize that you spent a month's worth of cash flow on fluff.

You need to get your message to the people who need solutions to a problem that's causing them some pain — people who can be educated to the possibilities you offer.

A problem-focused email approach gives you the advantage of connecting with an audience around a problem rather than trying to impress your way into their life.

Chapter 8
Five Essential Email Marketing Steps

Produce a continuous flow of prospects

It's been my experience that most lead generation programs are judged by the raw number of new contacts they produce. The bigger the fish bowl you brought home from the trade show, the happier you were with your participation.

Unfortunately, according to most analysis on the topic, well over half of those leads never come out of the fishbowl.

It's simply human nature. When you have a big stack of things, you have to put some aside to follow up later.

It reminds me though of that old line about leftovers.

"Should I throw these au gratins away now," your mother-in-law would ask after the big Sunday dinner, "or put them in the fridge for three weeks and then throw them away?"

 The same principle applies to a lot of the leads you get in stacks.

By applying the principles and discipline of good email marketing, you can develop a system that, at a minimum, supplements other programs that are working now. Interestingly, many organizations are finding that good email marketing can replace some of the legacy marketing that has become less effective.

And, critically important, the flow of leads is steady and predictable.

An email marketing system is the alternative to trade shows, road shows, and large advertising spreads.

The flow of leads is steady and predictable.

Throughout the year—day in, day out, week in, week out—your email marketing campaign sweeps the marketplace and serves up the most qualified, mature leads to your sales staff.

Think of it almost like a manufacturing facility where leads are processed in conveyor-belt fashion.

Names enter the process at the beginning, and thanks to a series of steps along the conveyor, they come out the other side as genuine prospects.

Virtually all of those prospects understand they have a problem they need to solve — they're at the top of the triangle.

The benefits that accumulate along the way include:

- Your cost per lead drops dramatically.
- You'll have better control of message content because you're not just letting somebody come to a website and kind of wander around.
- You're also going to have better utilization of your sales force because you'll be giving them pre-heated prospects who fit your target demographic and are ready to make a move. Your sales people have an abundance of opportunity, which keeps them sharp, motivated — and happy. There's lower turnover, less time needed to train new people.

Best of all, you — the business owner or manager — get a consistent, predictable, stable revenue stream.

Not to mention less drama and angst at the end of the quarter or year.

And today, that reduces the amount of crisis management you have to do — a welcome benefit to be sure.

Build a process that gets you "invited in"

The purpose of the email marketing system is to get the ready-to-act prospect to discriminate in your favor.

Rather than you calling up prospects and asking them to let you show them what you can do, you want prospects calling you and saying, "Will you help us with this?"

Obviously, you're better positioned when you've already established credibility with them and they believe you can solve the kind of problem they face.

Many attempts to use email in the pursuit of sales end in disaster because the misguided marketing person loses sight of the difference between being "invited in" and the quick sale.

This is especially true if you have a complex sales cycle. Closing the sale will, for some time to come, still rest squarely on the shoulders of your sales people.

But consider the advantage of putting them on the "right doorstep" with the right positioning.

Have them ring the bell
(Sort the wheat from the chaff)

One of the most important things to remember about an email marketing system is that it is a system.

It's not just about sending out a single email—it's the whole sequence.

You use a series of emails to find and qualify the best leads. And just as importantly, you can also disqualify people as you go along. You're able to detect characteristics that identify them as poor prospects.

So you're not wasting time with people who don't really have a problem, people who aren't really ready to buy, people who are just curious or "kicking tires."

It's kind of like the old carnival attraction where you swing a big hammer down on a pad and a weight flies up and rings the bell.

The people who come through this process are the ones who ring the bell. They've been carefully identified and qualified. They've demonstrated their "strength" as worthy prospects.

And once the process is in place, you bring people "down the conveyer line" automatically and systematically. You don't have to think about it. It's all happening in an orderly, consistent and regular fashion so prospects are popping out at the end of the line and ringing the bell.

Stay focused on the prospect's problem

In my consulting work, I frequently hear about the challenge of sales "dropping out of the funnel" (or off the forecast) just at the end of the quarter.

LASER BEAM

When this happens, it is usually because your sales process kicks into selling mode before the prospect is fully immersed in the weight and implication of their current business problem.

Any attempt to talk about yourself, your products, your services, or how great you are will bring the process to a quick — and unhappy — conclusion.

Be a trusted advisor... not an imposter

With all the downsizing I've seen the last few years, a lot of companies have started outsourcing. They no longer retain people in-house to research and develop programs and systems they'll need.

So, instead of buying products and services, now they have to buy solutions.

This forces them to think about things in a different way — frequently a way for which they are unprepared or unfamiliar.

I've seen companies buy a million dollars worth of hardware and software, then try to integrate it themselves, only to fail.

Other companies spend a million on hardware and software, then bring in someone from the outside to show them how to make it work. They've succeeded brilliantly.

Information on how to think about solving their problem, delivered by your email marketing system, establishes you as a credible source of information for the prospect.

Your stature grows even more if you can offer services like training and consulting as part of the package. The more ways you can help ensure that the overall business problem is solved, the more valuable you become.

As an email sequence progresses, the prospect will even begin to consider you a trusted advisor.

 Be on the lookout all along the way for opportunities to distinguish yourself from all the other vendors out there who contact the prospect with a product or service-centric approach. Seek linkage between what you do, and what the prospect needs to solve problems.

Remember that old saying. "Consumers don't buy products. They buy solutions."

You don't even have to have to command all the knowledge and information that's specific to their industry to position yourself as an important resource. You could go out and buy the expertise of industry insiders, then create a report to give to them.

Chapter 9
Keep the Process Moving

Risk is the major source of friction and delay in deals

Figuring out how to remove the risk your prospect perceives can be a critical component to almost any lead generation program.

The work on this topic by marketing genius Jay Abraham is probably the most clarifying on this and I would encourage you to seek out that information. The topic is too broad in scope to do it justice here.

That said, at every step of your email marketing system you want to employ tactics to take the perceived risk out of the process for your prospect.

And I'm not just talking about closing the sale, but every intermediate step as well.

You must be aware that when a prospect gives you an email address, in these days of abundant spamming, they are taking a risk. You can reduce the perception of risk by clearly disclosing that

- their name will not be sold,
- they will not receive information or sales pitches on subjects that are unrelated to their inquiry, and

- at any moment they can reliably remove their name from your email list and receive no more information.

In fact the goal is to create a bond of trust by so pleasantly surprising your prospect with the value and quality of the materials you send that they develop an affection for your emails and open them eagerly because they are of so much value.

The silver bullet—a "Champion Kit"

This topic is a notch or two off "dead center" when it comes to email marketing, but it is so compelling a leverage tool for email marketing plans that I would be doing you a disservice if I didn't mention it.

No matter how good your persuasion approach, no matter how proficient your sales people, there will be prospects that don't move toward a purchase when you would normally expect to close the deal.

Here's a strategy to help with that.

This strategy is called "the Champion Kit."

Used well, it can be your "Silver Bullet," accelerating your complex sales cycle.

When a prospect makes an investment in a product or service they typically have to gain a consensus that 1) the investment is worthwhile and 2) that your offering meets their criteria better than any other vendor.

In most cases this takes the form of written analysis.

In one typical client situation it included:

1. A written description of the problem to be solved.

2. A written description of solution alternatives with pros and cons.

3. A list of vendors that provide potential solutions.

4. A comparison of the various vendors in a matrix, with the desired features, and a check box next to each to indicate if that particular vendor had that particular feature.

5. A justification for selecting the chosen vendor, with a plan for purchasing and integrating the solution.

In my experience, I've found time and time again deals would stall in the analysis phase.

But once you understand it, you'll be able to develop a plan to overcome the stall.

One prospect told me it took about 120 to 160 hours of time to put together this kind of analysis — a daunting task, even though he had already made up his mind to buy my product.

My solution was to prepare those materials for him (on my time not his). I then gave him a copy for him to modify as he saw fit. The amount of time it took him to "analyze" his decision went from 120 to 160 hours down to about 10.

Putting it all together takes some time and effort on your part. But when you give it to the prospect, they can edit the material and take a certain amount of ownership in the outcome.

A side benefit is they get "kudos" for their comprehensive analysis from their peers.

Avoid self-centered Champion Kits

A champion kit should portray a credible point of view, even though you prepare it in the hope it will help swing a decision in your favor.

A vendor-centric package is immediately rendered completely useless.

Any appearance of self-promotion is self-defeating. Resist the temptation to picture all the benefits your product offers that your competition doesn't.

Your intention is to give the client a framework for making their decision.

So the kit has to be credible, and certainly will point (gently) to some flaws or weaknesses in your offering in the interest of credibility.

If your product doesn't fit a particular need, say so.

Because if you have an A+ in every box on the feature comparison, evaluation team members will blow off the materials as delusional.

Making the case for ROI

You've probably heard someone say that a few years ago, when the "New Economy" was roaring, that if you stuck your hand up in the air, an order flew into it.

Today, after the free-spending late 90s, in most companies the Chief Financial Officer is in the decision loop for any large purchase. If you're asking the prospect to spend more than $1,000, the CFO will probably review the decision.

So remember — you might be able to get the VP of Purchasing lathered up about your solution for emotional reasons. But you had better be able to put some positive numbers in front of the CFO if you expect to close the deal.

And every CFO will want to know "What's our return on investment?"

In other words, he or she wants to know the "ROI."

This is one of those opportunities for you to distinguish yourself as the trusted advisor.

If you can provide a tool in the form of a spreadsheet that shows the CFO how to determine ROI, you'll really set yourself apart from the competition.

You'll have to ask them a certain number of questions to formulate the spreadsheet. Run the numbers and present your findings. You'll be doing them a favor they won't soon forget — and you'll be doing them a service they probably won't get from your competition.

There are also a couple of benefits to you.

First, of course, you'll have heightened your rapport with the prospect.

Second, you'll be able to tell how favorably predisposed your prospect is to you by their willingness to answer your questions during the formulation.

Of course, you'll run into situations where they won't answer all your questions because of legal or proprietary reasons. In that case, just send them spreadsheet and let them plug in the numbers themselves.

By doing this, you can usually give them the key information they need to make a decision — and it's all simplified for them on a single page.

Chapter 10

Four Ways to Identify and Qualify Legitimate Prospects

Sweep your market for prospects

The metaphor here comes from the kind of radar you see on the television weather report.

You'll frequently see a line sweeping around the tube looking at all of your local area to uncover rain, snow, cloud build-ups, etc.

The important concept here is the sweep... because most companies don't "sweep" the entire potential market. They just look in pockets of the market and as a result they get a distorted picture.

I often hear from CEOs or sales vice presidents, "We win most deals we know about but there are a lot of them we don't hear about until it is too late." This is the classic symptom of a failure to "sweep."

Using direct mail and advertising, it used to be very expensive and somewhat labor-intensive to sweep the market... you could do it but it took a strong force of will to make it happen regularly.

In the early days of email marketing there were also problems with the "sweep." The lists were immature. As a result it was hard to target precisely. You would send a marginally irrelevant email to a bunch of addresses and then deal with all the negative consequences.

But, thankfully, things have changed.

Email lists have become much more precise and sophisticated in recent years, and thanks to their growing sophistication, it's possible to blanket an entire active marketplace with a good mailing list.

And here's some more good news.

You can use the same list more than once. You can typically mail the same list every 3 to 4 months and usually produce response rates similar to what you saw on your first mailing.

Does that sound counter-intuitive?

It makes sense if you think about it. Circumstances change dramatically from quarter to quarter… and the problem-focused email that was deleted before it was even opened three months ago is now more welcome and relevant.

The people on the list are all at different stages of need. Some might need you right away, some might need you soon, some might need you someday, and some will never need you.

But people don't stay in the same stage forever. So if you email your list every 90-120 days, in most cases, you'll find new people moving up into an interest stage. The same email they sent to the trash bin quickly three months ago now raises some interest.

Once you've identified a good list through your testing process, you can actually "sweep" your entire marketplace on a regular basis.

Three to four months between sweeps seems about right. Six months is probably too long.

Target for profitability

Even though you can get sharply segmented lists from brokers, you'll still need to test and refine them to target the people you want to reach most.

It's hard to anticipate what will work best when you're just starting. But through experience and experimentation you can zero in on the best potential prospects fairly fast.

This is one of those cases where lists are a much better starting point than leads you glean from your website. Anyone might land on your website and start downloading your information. But you don't know if it's Warren Buffett or a geek in the bowels of some dotcom company.

To maximize your initial testing it is critical (to your checkbook) to work with a very experienced list broker or list selection consultant.

The idea here is to test small until you build confidence. And only then, when you are assured of your desired result, do you roll out in large volumes.

An important rule of thumb is to never roll out to a list more that 5 times larger than the initial quantity tested.

For example let's say you test a 75,000 name list with a 5,000 name sample. You could roll out the results of your test to approximately 25,000 names on the list with confidence. Once that proved successful, you could then rollout to the balance of the list.

Can they be educated?

Unfortunately, even a great list won't tell you certain character or personality traits about a prospect.

You want to find somebody you can educate.

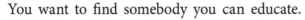

There are many people out there who will never buy your product, no matter how good it is, because you're not the market leader. This seems to be particularly true for entrepreneurs starting a business. They tend to opt out of email marketing programs.

Some people will show some interest in an email and download your white paper or report. But as soon as they find out you're not a marquee name or a big player in the industry, they ditch you. That's just as well.

If they're going to have preconceived notions or they're going to be hard to educate, your sales people will be wasting their time and you're better off without them. They're just going to clog up your sales process.

The people you want to work with have certain traits.

- They're problem focused.
- They don't buy into labels or "star power."
- They choose to get your information because they're curious or in pain.
- They're willing to disclose information about themselves or their situation.

Create an itch they have to scratch...

The key to good lead generation in a complex sales process is offering educational material your prospect finds so compelling that they can't pass up your report or white paper.

You want the prospect thinking, "If I don't get this, I might miss some information I need to know for a decision I'm going to have to make... and making that mistake could cost me prestige, my job, or my company a lot of money."

If somebody is considering an expensive product and you offer them a white paper listing the mistakes people make when they buy that type of expensive product — they have to get that white paper. Their job may be on the line, especially if it's a high ticket item and there's a lot riding on doing it right.

Chapter 11
The Rapport Sequence

The rapport sequence is the heart of the email marketing campaign.

It is also the part that most people get wrong on their first attempt.

 The ultimate goal is to build such a good relationship with the prospect that they invite you to help them solve their problem.

You have a lot more power in the process when that happens.

The rapport sequence features an automated series of emails that are sent out over time.

There are two questions you have to answer in creating the content for these documents.

"What should I say?"

"When should I say it?"

When you've figured out the correct answers to these questions, through experience and experiment, your rapport sequence will create a warm place for you in the hearts of your prospects.

The short term goal of the sequence is to build a bridge and a bond between you and the prospect. It could take weeks or months, depending on the complexity of your sales cycle.

But without the rapport sequence, it might never happen at all.

Above all, your communication in the rapport sequence needs to be sincere. It should have what I call "personal texture." People you deal with should get a sense they're communicating with a real person, as opposed to an electronic robot spewing out email responses.

It starts when you get their name and email address from a reputable, permission-based list owner. That indicates that they're open to getting information by email. They have a problem and they're looking for solutions.

Your subject line intrigues them enough to get them to be slightly vulnerable and open your email.

You offer a white paper or a free report. As they read, their interest rises. They're thinking, "Hmm, these people are saying something here. I might be able to solve my problem."

They download your white paper and maybe they start to read it.

 What often happens next could be discouraging, but it shouldn't be. The process allows for it. That's one of the beauties the process offers.

Shortly after they download your document, the phone rings, they spill their coffee and they're off onto a thousand other things and just that quickly, you've fallen "off their radar screen."

Your white paper may stay on their desk for a few days (or fly around on their desk unopened), and eventually they'll probably file it away somewhere, promising themselves they'll read it later. But they probably never will.

Research indicates that people rarely read much of the white papers they download. (In fact, you'd be amazed at how little they read of the books they buy. One major company that recently did a study on this subject discovered that most people who bought a book didn't read more than ten pages.)

So you usually have to follow up with more emails to reconnect them with their initial interest.

A well-designed rapport sequence re-enters their life through their inbox a number of times in the weeks or months that follow, seeking to raise their interest threshold again.

You continue to feed them a series of educational, informational pieces that amplify their interest or concern. If they keep responding, then you know they're serious about getting information. They're probably feeling some pain and they're looking for relief.

At every step of the process you are also giving them the option to never receive another email from you again… this is essential!

You keep the process going, gently and gradually. Usually, over time, your contacts accumulate. They either opt out or they ask for your help to buy.

The important thing is to keep contacting them, building rapport all along the way.

And one more time for emphasis — because this is a key concept many people miss.

Once someone has downloaded a report or a white paper, you know they're interested because they've crossed the first threshold, i.e., raised their hand.

Now you want to start finding out how much they're interested. So you start asking them to cross more thresholds.

After they've made that first request, it's a good idea to send an immediate message asking if they were able to download what they wanted.

You'll often get emails back from them saying something like, "Gee, you guys sure are working late tonight."

That's good. You want to send the message of competence, care, and concern. It shouldn't look too formal, and you might even want it to have a little personality.

Some people think all correspondence, especially marketing material, should be sanitized. I disagree.  Some personality in the communication process seems to work extremely well on the Internet.

In any case, the document they've downloaded is designed to test their curiosity by offering more "compelling reading."

For instance, offer links to click to request a spreadsheet or a follow-up mini-report of some kind.

You can construct the report in such a way that they'll indicate their level of interest. You might write about "Seven Fatal Mistakes," and at the end of each one, put a link that offers them information on how to avoid that particular mistake. When they click on that link another report or document arrives in their inbox moments later.

 You keep track of what they download and that tells you who's reading deeper into the white paper and which of the "fatal mistakes" is causing them the greatest concern. At that point, you're really beginning to separate "suspects" from "prospects" by detecting their level of interest.

You're also building up a database of information that your sales staff can use later in the process. It speaks volumes about your ability to help them solve their problem.

It gives you the power to start your first phone conversation with them "briefed."

And it engenders their appreciation (you're not starting at square one), and multiplies your chances of closing a sale because you are executing with knowledge and precision.

Five types of rapport sequence messages

Unfortunately many more companies simply *use* autoresponders than use them properly.

One autoresponse sequence I received recently went like this:

Message 1 — Hi, you should buy our product.

Message 2 — Hi, here are some more reasons we have a really great product.

Message 3 — Hi, not sure why you haven't bought our product yet… it really is the best product in the market.

Message 4 — Hi, we'll sell you our product for half price, but today only.

Message 5 — Boy are you lucky! We're extending our half price offer.

And on it goes… basically relentless sales message after sales message.

I've found that a rapport sequence should have a texture, rhythm and tempo to it so your prospect understands that you are interested in helping them solve their problem… and do it in a way that allows them the time and mental space to inhale and exhale.

There are five types of messages you can use in the rapport sequence and my experience is that all five should be used. The mix may vary, but all are an essential part of building rapport.

Transactional

You're asking a question like, "Did you get the report okay?" You're just demonstrating concern.

Educational

An educational message might read like this

"We had a few questions from people who read the white paper and one area that seemed to be unclear was … (fill in the blank). Here's the author's response to that question."

People like to get educational messages because they feel that they're being kept informed.

Sales Pitch

Okay, as long as you do it with some subtlety. After rapport has been built you can get by with saying something like, "This may or may not be of value to you. I'll leave it to you to decide… our CEO has authorized a 20% discount on any order received before such-and-such a date. We are offering this to meet certain sales levels in this quarter. And if  you're able to, and want to take advantage of this discount, please reply to this email and I'll send you the details."

Enticement

You can notify someone of an event you're participating in and even invite them to join you.

"Hey," you could say, "we're going to be at the industry tradeshow in booth number 64. We hope you'll stop by."

Hygiene

Even though you've done everything right all along, you'll still have some prospects who have received a long sequence of emails from you, downloaded some or all of your information, and seemed to be interested — but have never bought.

It's time to ask them if they want to stay in the process. You send them an email asking something like, "Is what we're doing helping you in any way? We don't want to keep sending you emails if we're not being helpful to you, and we respect your right to privacy. We all get too many emails. Please unsubscribe from our lists if you don't find this terrifically valuable."

Some will unsubscribe, of course. But you'll be amazed at the responses you'll get from others. You'll get people who'll say, "No. No. Don't take me off the list!"

My experience tells me to be very selective about sending sales messages. But send lots of transactional messages.

There's something about the interplay that tends to make the prospect connect with you — someone who cares about their problems and might have a solution for what the problems they're trying to solve.

How to guarantee your rapport sequence will fail

The most common reason a rapport sequence fails is premature selling.

We live in a commercial world and we're used to hearing everyone talk about how great they are or all the wonderful things their product will do.

We'd naturally be tempted to think that's how an email marketing process should start too.

But, as one well-known commercial campaign tells us… "Not exactly."

In fact, not at all.

A good rapport sequence has a pace — a tempo that resonates with the prospect.

What you say is important. You talk at first about your prospect's problem and ways to solve it. You do not talk about your company or your product.

 When you say it is equally important. Say too much too soon, and you'll fail as badly as if you said nothing at all.

The biggest challenge in sculpting any rapport sequence is detecting that tempo.

At some point of course, the discussion between you and the clients must turn from "What's the problem?" to "What's the solution?"

You can begin to do that kind of thing after they've received five to eight emails from you and they're likely to be receptive to it. They realize by that point that you're not going to just jump down their throat and try and sell them something. By then they should have a certain amount of confidence that you're going to offer them valuable information.

This is where they begin to think of you as an advisor.

This is where they invite you in to help.

This is where the face-to-face relationship begins to advance the ball.

A well-designed and executed rapport sequence is like a pitch down the middle of the plate for your sales people. It gives them a great opportunity to knock the ball out of the park.

Chapter 12
Eighteen Essential Components Simplified

This chapter will give you an overview of the main elements of a program.

As with all systems, there will be slight variations in how you adapt this to your situation. But a good grasp of what follows will serve you well.

At a fundamental level, an email lead generation system consists of five essential elements.

Just like a direct mail program, you have:

1. An offer letter.
2. A list.
3. A piece of educational material to provide.
4. A system for capturing names.
5. A system for sending out follow-up messages.

Remember, this is not a get-rich-quick program.

It's a way to build a step-by-step process that will produce revenue automatically and systematically, consistently and predictably.

When you first look at the detail of an email marketing system, your eyes may glaze over.

The process looks complex and there's likely to be some unfamiliar technology involved. Keep in mind that's probably how people felt about using the telephone a hundred years ago.

In this chapter, I'm going to take some of the mystery and techno-mumbo-jumbo out of it.

Here's what you'll need

Technology

Before you do anything, you have to know what technology you need, and whether you already have it or not. This is where a lot of people stumble.

You need an email infrastructure. It can be relatively simple and cost you less than $200 a month. It can be sophisticated and cost you $10,000 a month. The important thing is to determine what fits your needs and put it in place.

Next, buy a list and do a mailing.

All of a sudden you may get five hundred emails bouncing back into your collection system, and you don't know what to do next.

Here are the steps to follow:

Do a "Sales Diagnostic Survey"

The first thing you hear from companies that are trying email marketing for the first time is, "I don't want spend a lot of money only to find out that this doesn't work."

There are some businesses and products and services that should not be marketed through email because the lists haven't been developed yet, or for any number of other reasons I won't elaborate on here.

So it's very important to test to make sure you're doing the right thing.

But it's becoming the right thing for more and more companies. The lists are getting so much better. Just a few years ago you'd spend days, weeks, or months hunting down a decent email list. Now it seems like there are five different lists that target most audiences.

You can use a kind of check list if you're doing this on your own. You'll want to know if you've done good market research. Do we have proper legal content? Do we have a legitimate list broker?

Again, people are focused on their pains, not on your products or services.

So it's very important to emphasize the pains that they're having and accurately estimate the financial impact of those pains. That's critical for the design of your outbound persuasion piece and the report that you use as follow-up.

Decide on a budget

You can decide on just about any budget. Entry costs are very low. Try a couple of experiments as long as you track the results.

You don't have to drop a bundle of money into a test before you're smart enough to tune up the process and realize some significant gains.

Put a plan together with dates

Focus on making things happen in a certain time period. Hold yourself accountable because the hard part is setting up the system and launching it. Once you've done that, you'll be delighted at the things that you don't have to worry about in order to get prospects knocking on your door.

Compose an outbound email

This will be the first thing the prospect gets from you. It's critical that you do it right, because if you don't you'll kill your chances of getting the results you want.

You can do nine things well and only two things poorly and the net result will still be failure.

Copywriting

You can get professional copywriting. But many entrepreneurs and business owners can be coached to write good copy themselves. They certainly understand the benefits of their products better than an outsider.

Either way, the copy must be compelling. You want to create that itch they have to scratch. Ask yourself, "What can I write to get their mouse finger to move a quarter of inch when they get down to the link in the letter?" That's all you're trying to accomplish at the moment.

Just ask for one action. Present a single opportunity.

At this stage, avoid talking about your products or your company. Focus on the prospect. Once again, the short-term goal is to get somebody to raise their hand and say, "Hey, I have this problem." The long term goal is to get your sales person invited in as a trusted advisor.

Be sure to focus on the trouble the prospect is having, and particularly the financial impact that problem is creating. Sometimes you can be direct and say you know that their problem is costing them $25,000 dollars per incident and they're probably experiencing three incidents per week. With others you have to be a little bit more subtle. But either way, the financial impact is ultimately what's going to move somebody to action.

Use a quality list

This is extremely important.

When you're testing you want to make sure that you're talking to the right audience.

A lot of people have spent a lot of money perfecting their persuasion approach and then have tried to save money by renting a cheap list.

They didn't know if their persuasion approach worked or not because they didn't put it in front of the right people.

Keep in mind that people put their names on a list for a variety of reasons. Some websites offer incentives, like free MP3 players or mobile phones. They may not be even remotely interested in the topic of your outbound email, but their names show up on cheap lists.

Some lists key on job titles. They'll cull all the vice presidents or the COO's or the CFOs.

As I mentioned, the assumption that you need to talk to a vice president isn't as sound as it used to be. Often you'll do better with a passionate advocate at a lower management level — someone who's really hot on getting your solution into their company.

Test your lists with a pilot program

At minimum, you should test about 3,000 names. That will give you a pretty good idea whether your persuasion approach works.

And again, never roll out more than five times your test amount. If you test 3,000 names and you get a 2.5% response, you can be relatively sure that emailing to 15,000 names will probably produce the same result.

You want to validate that the subsequent materials that you're sending them have the intended persuasion consequence. You want to validate the rapport sequence. You want to validate the conversion process and you want to convert those people that become clients to referral sources, and that's another very important part of your total email design. And if you haven't taken that into account, you've missed a big part of the value of an email system.

But you never want to test a list, get a 2.5% response and then roll it out to 50,000 names. You'll do better to split it up into three different mailings over a period of three weeks. Circumstances change quickly, events ebb and flow, flukes occur. You want to be careful not to bet the whole farm on one giant mailing at one time.

Where to buy your lists

There are mail list brokers who are reliable providers. Edith Roman is probably the best known.

Associations all have lists, of course, but not all will sell them to you. Sometimes you have to get creative.

One company wanted to buy an association list. The association refused because it was a non-profit and was concerned about the perception of spamming.

Well it turned out that the association had a book club that was managed by a company that ran book clubs for associations.

The book club had a list — and was willing to sell it.

So there are ways to tiptoe around and get a certain list if you think it's a really good one.

Think of lists the way a wildcatter thinks of oil fields.

Drill in one place and nothing happens.

Drill in another, and you get a little.

Drill in yet another and you hit a gusher.

Lists tend to work like that too.

That's why testing is so important.

The most powerful and effective list is an "endorsed" list. This is where someone sends an email recommending you.

These usually happen as a result of pre-existing relationships or networking.

Test copy that's exactly the same

Test enough to get statistically reliable results. Only then should you start testing changes and recording results.

Keep in mind that whenever you send out a mailing, you're doing well if 30% to 40% of the recipients open it — no matter what the subject line says. So you may actually send four or five emails to the same person before they read your message.

Look for problems first

There are business owners who are pursuing positive goals: faster growth, bigger market share, a higher stock price. They tend to be less responsive than people who are in pain and looking for relief.

You'll do better if you "accentuate the negative," so to speak — at least at first. Problems seem to trigger action faster than opportunities. Economic uncertainty, industry evolution, technological change — the sort of disruption or displacement that causes anxiety will motivate people to move.

So you want to look for situations where people have to do things differently than they did before.

Data capture is a critical component

You already have the person's email address from
your list, but you want them to give it to you again.
That's how they raise their hand. That's how you
know they have a problem.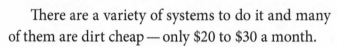

There are a variety of systems to do it and many
of them are dirt cheap — only $20 to $30 a month.

They're hosted on the web, so you don't have to set anything up
on your own computer. In fact, you shouldn't keep a list on your own
computer because if it crashes and you haven't backed it up, you lose
your entire investment in the lead generation program.

"From" and "Subject" lines in your outbound email

This is the crucible — the total success or failure of your email
program hinges on how you look at this point.

If your message doesn't get opened it's all for naught.

And the number one way people decide if they're going to
open an email is by asking themselves, "Do I know who or where it
came from?"

60% to 70% of the decision to open comes from the name.

Use a real name — somebody who actually works for the company.
Otherwise you risk some legal jeopardy.

If they see a person's name, they'll generally reserve judgment for
a moment.

 Be careful though, because when you put some-
one's name on an email and then send it out to a
quarter of a million people, you'll get some crazy — and
threatening — responses. Use someone's maiden name
or a middle name, so somebody can't look them up in
a directory and show up at their house.

First names alone don't get as good a response as first and last names together. Most spammers are using single first names, and most people have already caught on to it. We're all getting pretty sophisticated at filtering out email we don't want to read because we're getting so much of it.

In testing, women's names work better than men's. Anglo Saxon Protestant names worked better than non-Anglo names. Common names work better than uncommon ones. A "Betty Smith" would work better than say "Martina Okolona" because you're more likely to say to yourself, "I think I know someone named Betty Smith... is she the woman I met at that seminar last month?"

These are all things that have been measured over the last few years and they consistently work best for getting through that first filter that people have.

If the reader gives you the benefit of the doubt on the name, the next thing they glance at is the subject line.

Keep it short

A subject line is, in effect, a headline. You can write a great headline. But if they can't see it, it doesn't do you any good. Most people have their screen constrained so they can't see the entire subject line. They're just looking a piece of it. So it's very important to design your message to fit in as short a space as possible.

A twenty-character width is about all you really have.

Keep this in mind too — a while back, some lawmakers were talking about anti-spam legislation that required the letters "ADV" or "ADV:ADLT" (for "advertising" or "advertising: adult") in the subject line of unsolicited email.

The CAN-SPAM legislation killed that idea, but you never know when the next challenge to permission-based opt-in email is going to come.

That's why I encourage renting the better lists, because you're getting people that have said they definitely want the information.

You'll always get someone who accuses you of spamming if you send out thousands of emails. But people on the good lists generally know why they're getting an email from you, and they don't mind.

Landing pages

When a reader opens your email, reads it, and clicks on a link, they're taken to a "landing page."

Don't be tempted to put a lot of flash and pop on a landing page.

Research shows they work best if you keep them light on graphics and heavy on the promise of problem solving.

Again, all you want them to do is one thing, one action, one step: to type in their name and their email address and click "Submit."

That gives them access to the information they're looking for.

About 25% to 30% of the people won't do it because they don't want to give away their email address.

Or sometimes they'll give their company email address or even a "throw-away" account at Yahoo or Hotmail.

Here's something else that you must understand about the Internet.

You never know what it's going to do.

Thanks to technological glitches, firewalls, spam filters, viruses, weather, and each individual PC's capabilities, it's hard to be certain if it's working on both ends at any given moment.

So you want to put in a couple of safety nets for people who can't get the document they want by filling out a form on your landing page.

Create a toll-free number and/or offer to send out the document by mail.

The "incentive:" what you should offer them

These are the things you offer in your outbound email to entice somebody into your persuasion process. An outbound email that offers an educational report or a white paper works very well. I know companies that have used the same one for several years and it works great. A well written white paper that's specifically targeted will work for a long time.

A white paper, of course, is a document that is written to describe a certain topic. The term "white paper" sounds scholarly, and that's what you want if you're sending to a technically-oriented market.

You might then use the word "report" for other segments of your market because that's better known to them and sounds a little more "user-friendly."

Your outbound email could also offer something as simple as a transcribed interview. You don't need to go to extremes producing it. Transcribed interviews work extremely well if you're working on a deadline and you need to come up with something to offer in a hurry.

Check lists have also tested well. Lists of resources, access to online video or audio screenings, and so on, can be offered in an outbound email and they will attract people.

Finally, remember this important point: one offer per email only. Don't start giving them multiple choices. You don't want to say, "Well, we have a white paper and if you'd like, you can also hear a recording of our last seminar..."

Responding to leads

Once someone raises their hand and asks for more information, an automated chain of events is set into motion.

When the system receives a request for information, a sequence of "autoresponders" triggers. Autoresponders manage and facilitate the responses to the people coming in.

Automation, of course, is the key. In fact, it would probably be impossible without it.

But don't jump right into a fully automated system.

You need to test it to make sure everything is working as it should — and that takes some human oversight.

Somebody has to look at every email that goes out and every one that comes in as the filters are set up. Do that manually and pump a couple of tests through the system until you're satisfied that all the responses are being handled properly.

 Create a safety net by designating one person to be the chief communications officer for the project. It could be somebody in your company or it could be a consultant you hire. Put them in charge of responding to emails that come in from the system.

Wait a minute. I said this whole process was automated, didn't I?

Anytime you do a program you might have 10% to 20% of the total volume of leads that come in that might require a reply the autoresponders aren't programmed to provide.

A very important part of developing that relationship with somebody is promptly handling their question. Sometimes it takes a live human being to do that.

There are, of course, some pitfalls any time you deal with technology. Accidents and flukes happen. For instance, when two autoresponders somehow get connected to each other, they can wind up sending each other the same message hundreds of times, just bouncing back and forth. So make sure your filters are set up very precisely.

Tracking

When you send out your first email to someone, you want to be able to know whether they've opened it or not. There's automation available to do this and it's a helpful statistic to monitor.

But don't put too much faith in it.

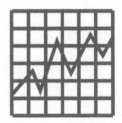

Some of the more popular email viewers like MS Outlook and Eudora have a preview screen. Anything that appears in the preview screen counts as an "open."

So it appears that someone cared enough to open the message, but it's very possible they didn't.

Tracking statistics is important in a lot of ways. But when all is said and done, one statistic counts more than any other: how many people bought what you're selling?

Chapter 13

Six Creative Vehicles You'll Need to Accelerate the Process

As I mentioned previously, the number of companies that provide lists has accelerated in the last few years. Like the dotcoms of a few years ago, many have come and many have gone. So you have to be careful where you're getting the names of the people you're going to email.

Offline lists

Again, someone who has a good list typically will not sell it to you; they will rent it. So that's the first way to separate the good from the bad. Stay with vendors like "Edith Roman" or "List Incorporated." Companies like "Cahners Publications" and "Penton's Publications" can separate names for you  in a number of different categories like geographical or job title. So you can buy every vice president within 50 miles of you, for example.

The offline list business is a mature industry. It's grown fairly sophisticated and you can find reputable companies with a long history and an excellent track record.

Online lists

Get ready to ride the rodeo pony when you start dealing with online list companies. It's very much the Wild West and you have to be extremely careful. There are still a lot of people preying on the ignorance of the "newbie." Typically, the fast-buck artists want to sell you a list.

Special deals for lists

One client tells me that he's enjoyed some success getting lists from magazines he advertises in. He buys advertising in several trade publications. He usually asks if they'll sell or rent their subscriber list to him as part of the bargain.

Usually they won't. But he reports that occasionally if a magazine really wants your business, they'll do it.

Articles

Sometimes you don't have to buy a list to get a persuasion piece in front of a target audience. If you're going after, say, the subscribers of a certain trade publication, you can propose writing an article for them. Some magazines don't accept outside contributions, but many — especially those with small staffs and tight budgets — are always on the lookout for good free material.

Of course, it can't be blatantly self-promotional. But contributing an article certainly helps position you as an expert and gives you immediate credibility. Most magazines will allow you to include a "resource box" which includes your contact information and even a link or two.

Joint venture partners

The Internet makes it easy to find potential partners thanks to a tool called "Alexa" at www. alexa.com. It's a company owned by Amazon that puts a small toolbar on your browser. Alexa helps you find sites that get a lot of traffic in your niche by showing you where certain sites rank numerically.

For instance a site that's ranked around number 10,000 gets about 40% more traffic than a site ranked 14,000.

You can use alexa.com to verify the traffic a site or a company is attracting. It helps you make a more intelligent decision about where to focus your efforts and resources when you're seeking joint venture (JV) partners.

Backward links

You can also click on a portion of the toolbar and it will tell you every site that links to the site you're looking at. This can be extremely helpful in scouting out prospective JV possibilities. You can bring up your biggest competitor's site and find out who's linking to them. If it's a company that complements you, or is in the same industry, you may want to consider partnering up with them.

Google offers something similar. You type "link:" and then you put a URL after it.

For example, "link:www.examplecompany.com." Google gives you a list of the sites that link to that URL. That's another way to find joint venture partners.

Of course, after you spot a website that looks like it has joint venture potential, you have to get in touch with the owners of the site. That can be time-consuming if you just go to the site and start poking around looking for contact information.

That's where the "Whois" (pronounced WHO IS) database can come in very handy.

Whois allows you to place a URL in a search box, and when you click enter, it will tell you who owns the domain and usually, how to contact them. It's a great timesaver.

"Whois," though, has become somewhat fragmented lately and isn't as simple to use as it used to be. So you might want to use a similar tool called "Cool Whois," which helps you select the correct "Whois" database to check.

Alexa also offers "The Wayback Machine," which is an archive of every site on the Internet going back a number of years.

You can see what someone's site used to look like on certain given dates in the past.

It has some interesting legal ramifications, but it's mainly helpful from a competitive standpoint. You can go back and see how your competition's website evolved and see what changes they've made.

That can indicate what they were doing that worked, and what didn't. That's good intelligence to have.

If you really like to get into the technical side of site building, you can even investigate how they used their metatags. Sometimes that will tell you their search engine strategy and a number of other useful things.

Who's in charge? The technical demands of an email marketing process can try the patience of most marketing people. So you'll probably have to make a decision about who implements and directs all the "techie" stuff.

Do you do it in-house, or outsource it? These are judgment calls you'll have to make along the way.

Chapter 14

Seven Damaging Mistakes Many Executives Make

Often in my consulting, I'll be called into a situation where a company has tried unsuccessfully to use email to grow the business.

Their effort was very good but one or two small "defects" in their materials poisoned the results.

Often, success is just a matter or removing or changing the offending elements.

If you've already done an email marketing campaign (or are doing one now), you can quickly look through these seven items and guess the impact any one may have had on your campaign.

 Second, if you're new to email marketing, you can use them as a checklist of things to avoid. I suggest reading the section now, but also putting a note on your calendar so you can come back and re-read it prior to launch.

Making just one of the mistakes that follow can mean the difference between a successful campaign and an unsuccessful one.

Confusing lead generation with sales

To be successful selling on the Internet, you first have to understand that "lead generation" and "sales" are two different things.

The sole purpose of a lead generation system is to get you in front of the right person at the right time: when they're ready and able to buy. They have a problem and they believe you might be the right person to help them solve it.

You know that because 1) they've allowed you to engage them all through the process and 2) they've invited you in — so they must believe that you can do them some good.

Most sales people love to talk to prospects like that, rather than prospects who may have just been surfing the web and stumbled across you through a search engine.

An email marketing system is designed to separate the serious prospects from the cyber-tirekickers.

Using your company website for your email campaign

It seems counter-intuitive. You want to brand yourself by using your company's name every chance you have, right?

Not in this case. At least not in my opinion.

Somebody reading your persuasion letter will look at the domain name and recognize it (or think they do).

They'll say, "Oh, this the ABC Company. I already know about them and what they do. They don't have anything to offer."

By comparison a problem-oriented or issue-focused domain name seems to work best.

A second reason not to use your main website is spam. Sooner or later, even if you are very careful to use opt-in lists, somebody who received your email will report you as a spammer (after forgetting they opted in).

Your ISP could shut down your site before you can work with the list owner to prove the accuser was on a permission list.

If that site is your main company site, all your traffic gets the "server not found" message instead of the relatively smaller number that are going to your website.

Here's something else that will seem counter-intuitive: you don't want everyone to find you.

 Unlike most websites on the Web, yours shouldn't be optimized for search engines. You don't want "tire-kickers" just stumbling across it.

You only want very directed traffic from the opt-in lists you purchase. Remember, you'll eventually be investing your quality sales time in these people, and you don't want to waste it on low-level leads that wander in after finding you with a search engine.

You also don't want your competitors copying it.

That's one of the disadvantages of most traditional marketing vehicles: they're transparent. If you ran a successful trade journal ad or TV commercial, your competition could analyze it, figure out why it worked, and then do something similar.

But if it's not on your main website, there's less chance they'll find it.

It gives your email campaign a "stealth" quality with respect to your competitors.

And that's good.

Using a bad list

Good lists usually don't come cheap.

Many smart Internet marketers have learned that it's not how many people you send to, it's how many people who buy.

Relatively tiny lists of highly targeted, highly motivated prospects often outperform mega-lists with hundreds of thousands of names.

Here's what to look for (and avoid) in a bad list:

- You'll get millions of names at once.
- It only costs a few cents per name (between $100-200 for the whole thing is typical).
- Someone offers them as a "weekend special" or something similar.
- You get a lot of hype like "this can't miss!"

I know of one entrepreneur who once thought he made a "great deal" on a list. He bought it for about $10,000 from an individual who assured him it was good.

However, the list turned out to be a random collection of emails.

 When he sent out his initial document, he was stunned by the negative response. This "blowback," went far beyond nasty notes that included a lot of words besides "unsubscribe." He was actually accused of spamming and was subsequently shut down by his Internet service provider.

In the end, that "bargain" list wound up costing him a lot more than the $10,000 he paid for it.

So be sure you deal with a reputable broker. They document where the names on the list came from so you can prove to your ISP that you're not spamming.

Most good list brokers won't sell you their lists. You can only rent them.

One final point to keep in mind before I leave this topic: a mediocre email or offer, sent to a good list, will usually get better results than a good one sent to a mediocre list.

Using "poison language"

I talked in Chapter 11 about selling too soon. It's a huge no-no.

But even if you're not blatantly selling or promoting yourself, you can use certain words in your emails that damage your chances of building the relationship you want.

Call these words "poison language," if you will, because you can bet they will turn off recipients and kill any chance of getting a good response.

What are the biggest offenders?

Words like "I," "we," and "our."

Software has been developed that actually reads through copy and counts the "I's" and "we's" and the "our's" in documents. That's called "company-centric" copy, and it tends to diminish response because it inspires people to dislike you.

Mentioning your company name and/or product early in the process tends to be counterproductive.

Don't invite a prospect to a product demonstration without explaining what it does, how it's used, and who it benefits.

Certain words automatically sound like hype, and you should avoid them. Stay away from superlatives like "the best," "the greatest," "the latest," or industry-leading.

It's always good to have a competent proofreader — someone who understands poison language — read your document before it goes out.

Formatting is also extremely important. I've seen people spend thousands to have an outbound email written, only to have it flop because they didn't pay attention to formatting. When they improved the format, they saw much higher response rates.

Long sentences and block paragraphs intimidate the reader — especially at the beginning. The most effective emails usually start with a friendly salutation followed by a quick, attention-getting one-sentence hook.

People don't like to start reading with their eyes right up against the edge of the screen.

Leave five spaces blank on the left side.

Double space. Use dividers like dashed lines, centered text, or text on an irregular margin.

Doing things that mildly disrupt normal scanning patterns will hold a reader's attention more effectively.

Give them multiple opportunities to click on a link throughout your email. Three links seem to work best.

If someone truly has a problem, and is highly motivated to solve it, they want to get as much information from your email as they can. This has been tested and proven to be correct over and over.

Long emails seem to work better than short ones. Most people find this hard to believe, but it's true. And if "most people" did a few simple tests, this would have been proven early on.

Don't overuse graphics and HTML. You're always doing a balancing act in the rapport sequence.

You want your emails to look professional so you're taken seriously. On the other hand, you want them to have a personal feel.

When you send your emails in HTML and add graphics, they certainly look more professional. But they also lose some of the personal "feel" that can be decidedly helpful in closing the sale.

I believe that a plain text message without graphics, from a person (not a company), is most likely to get opened first. Studies have shown this time and time again. People open their inbox and go down the list looking for real names — not company names.

I talked earlier about how some people think a dazzling website with a lot of pictures and swirling effects and audio will impress the visitor into buying the product. Similarly, there are a lot of people who believe spicing up an email message with graphics and HTML is the way to go.

I still believe "personal" is more important than "pretty." And this is true even if they've already opted into your list, moved along the rapport sequence, and in a sense, become "friends" with you.

Your company's image doesn't suffer as a result.

Also keep in mind that we're now living in a world that not only filters out spam and viruses, but also eliminates pop-ups, graphics, and anything else that might look like a sales message.

So while graphics and HTML emails look great "on the drawing board," they often become invisible by the time they hit the prospect's inbox.

You might be thinking right now, "How about giving people a choice somewhere in the sequence? If they want to receive messages with graphics and HTML, why not give them what they want?"

Well, mainly because it introduces a new variable. Ask a lot of people if they want "text only" or "HTML" and they'll say something like, "Well, you know… text I guess. I don't know what HTML is." A confused mind jeopardizes the sales process.

There are exceptions, of course, especially in certain industries where visual appeal is important — software comes to mind — but as a general rule it's probably better to stick with plain text.

People buy from people they know, like, and trust. Plain text generates those feelings more effectively than graphics and HTML.

Sending your emails at bad times

What you send is important.

When you send it is almost as important — and in some cases, it might even be more so.

Schedule your outbound email when it has the least competition from distractions:

- Don't send email on Monday or Friday.
- Don't send the day before a holiday or the first day back after a holiday.
- Don't send on an election day.
- Morning arrivals tend to get the best responses. The email should be seen as a "recent arrival" to the inbox.

- Tuesday, Wednesday, and Thursday mornings are good.
- Don't send if a disaster is in progress, or a riveting news event is capturing everyone's attention.

You can't always anticipate the best timing. But as a general rule try to avoid times when people have other things on their minds. You just don't want to be in somebody's hair during a terrorist attack or some kind of other emergency that's consuming their attention or causing them anxiety.

Be careful not to fall for "opportunities" to get lists from brokers during those times either.

A number of disreputable vendors offered discount rates on mailing to their lists after the attacks in September 2001, hoping to catch some people who would say, "Oh gee, we can save 50% on so and so list if we go with it next week."

In cases like that, you might think you're saving money, but you're actually wasting it. You'll get a very low response rate.

Asking for too much information too soon

Early in the process, all you want from them is their name and email address. If you ask for more than that, they're going to suspect that a sales process is under way, and that you're going to start bombarding them with sales messages moments after they click the "Submit" button.

Later on in the sequence you can come back and ask them for more information. Offer them a hard copy of something that needs to be mailed out — that's how to get their address.

If they stick with you through eight or nine emails, you can probably ask them for their phone number.

It's extremely important to keep it simple with senior level executives. They tend to be slower at operating a keyboard so they're not going to sit there and fill in a lot of blanks.

Generally, your best prospects are those who *will* sit there and fill in a lot of blanks — but it's best to let them do it later in the process.

Don't be tempted to underestimate someone who has a Gmail, Hotmail, Yahoo! or AOL address. There's a latent suspicion among people who do business on the Internet of folks who use those email services. The thinking is, "they're using a cheap email service so they're probably not a prospect…"

In fact, some very highly placed executives use web-based email addresses because they don't want to give their "real" address to a stranger. If they're interested, and you move them through the process properly, their real address will surface eventually.

Web-based email addresses are sometimes referred to as "throwaways," or, in some circles, "crap-catchers."

One caveat here. There are some people who will fill out anything you put in front of them. I've nicknamed them "See Mores," because no matter how much information you offer, they always want to "see more."

If they're taking time to fill out a lot of blanks, they probably don't have anything better to do. They make poor prospects because they clog up the sales process.

Offering "bribes"

Conventional Internet wisdom says you should give things away whenever you can. You might be tempted to give away some kind of freebie on the landing page.

Think twice before you do. You don't want anything distracting from the process.

If you still insist on giving something away, make sure it's related to the problem you're trying to solve.

Some companies have attempted to gather email addresses by offering gadgets or other enticements.

Generally these leads tend to be low quality — *very* low quality.

A contest with a prize poses another danger.

One entrepreneur of my acquaintance raffled off an expensive automobile. He collected thousands of email addresses, and his sales force started following up.

Each person who was called by a company representative immediately assumed they were being notified they had won the car.

They were disappointed when they discovered that was not the case.

Some were downright angry, moments later, when they figured out someone was now trying to sell them something.

Very few of these "leads" turned into sales.

 That said, it's generally okay to offer a free audio cassette or a CD sometimes during the rapport sequence, as long as it's a genuine resource or good information that will help the prospect solve their problem. That's not really a bribe.

Raffle tickets, gadgets, free vacations and other such things are bribes. I suggest you avoid them.

And also...

There's one other danger that really isn't part of the email marketing process, but can make it appear that the process didn't work.

It happens often with young companies that haven't yet refined and perfected the closing. They haven't really figured out how to "sell" their product, or at least how to present their product's benefits so they're apparent to prospects.

Thisofcourse,canleadtounsuccessfulclosesandunsatisfactorylead-to-sale ratios.

When that happens, there will be a temptation to blame the system for "not providing solid leads" or "not qualifying prospects sufficiently."

So if that happens, take care to analyze the situation carefully and find the real reason for your lack of success.

Chapter 15

Eight Indispensable "Fast Track" Strategies

How to shorten your time to success

The learning curve can be long and steep for those coming to email marketing for the first time. The same holds true for those "battle-scarred" souls who have tried it and not met with success.

In my experience there are a few things you can do to move the ball down the field a little faster.

What follows are my eight secrets for improving your odds, reducing your pain, and helping you get the jump on your competition.

Transcribe sales people

Your sales people probably represent your best source of copy when you're writing your outbound email, free report or white paper. They're out talking to customers everyday, solving their prospects' problems, and explaining their product's benefits. Ask them questions and transcribe their responses.  You'll have to do a little editing for grammar and usage, of course. But in most cases, you'll be able to use their language almost verbatim.

Paradoxically... never, ever ask your sales person to write copy for you. That skill uses a completely different part of their mind — and probably requires some formal (or at least comprehensive, self-guided) training and study.

Use the best lists

I keep coming back to this, don't I? It's very easy to be penny-wise and dollar-dumb when it comes to lists. You want to avoid as much guesswork as possible, and using high quality, narrowly targeted lists helps you do that.

These lists cost more money, but in the long run, they're more productive.

You can absolutely test yourself to success by ensuring you are talking to the right target audience... when you use a weak list you introduce too many variables to provide meaningful results.

Segment or bracket?

The question sometimes comes up, "Should you segment your prospects tightly from the start, focusing only on the people at the top of the Triangle of Hidden Opportunity?"

Or should you "bracket" prospects, trying to pull in some of the ones who are on the fringes?"

The answer depends on the product, the company, and the situation.

The more complex the decision, the more people are likely to be involved in the decision-making process.

Suppose, for instance, you're selling software and its application touches several different parts of the organization.

You can send a problem-focused email to each part of the organization, hoping to find one person (or more) who says, "Hey, this could be our solution."

Conversely, if your product is targeted strictly at aircraft machine shop owners, your best bet is likely to be focused only on them.

Be careful with graphics

Graphics are another subject I've already touched on, but here's an additional thought to mull over.

Used appropriately, graphics can help break up long documents — especially white papers and reports.

There are 7 concepts you must grasp to work with graphics effectively in the context of lead generation:

1. Nobody starts at the beginning and reads through to the end... most business people "Swiss cheese" their reading, flipping through the material, reading in snippets and sections while on hold or waiting for planes.
2. Given that they do this, a long report of page after page of text will rarely be read because the reader has a hard time finding an "entry point."
3. Graphics create that entry point... and dispersed throughout your material create many friendly entry points.
4. But flashy, professional graphics send the wrong message. "We're big and important and you are lucky we are writing this for you." So

save your graphic artist for your main website and your company brochure — because letting them touch your lead generation is a recipe for disaster.

5. One of my secrets is using "rustic" graphics (like those in this book)… the ones that get you to think, "What the hell could that graphic have to do with this topic?"

6. That has the power effect of pulling the reader from the friendly graphic into the text, just to figure out how the twisted mind of the author can reconcile the text with the graphic.

7. And the "trick" that makes this all work is using a graphic without a caption. A caption lets the reader off the hook… they don't have to look at the text to figure out what point the graphic is intended to make.

Experience tells me you might want to re-read this section before you launch your campaign… This is one of the areas where someone new to email marketing is most likely to stumble.

Don't waste time and resources gathering extensive statistics

Some techies and geeks get really wrapped up in statistics that mean very little in the long run. They talk about how long a visitor stays on your website, how many emails are opened versus not opened, and a lot of other things that have very little impact on your bottom line.

Track what matters — the things that lead

to sales: how many people clicked the last link? Numbers like that mean business. Those are the stats that count.

Be especially careful about an over-focus on pure volume of activity and response rates.

A low response rate that produces a lot of good prospects and eventual sales is obviously preferable to a high response rate that does the opposite.

Test, test, and test some more

You don't have to lose money tuning your results. You can test in small quantities. Try a little bit. Measure, and watch what happens. Test a little bit more. Test a little bit more. Patterns will clearly emerge that you can use to improve your response rate.

The biggest horror stories I've heard come from people who put together a plan and then jump in too fast and too big. You'll hear them say things like, "I bought this 50,000-name list for $7,000 and I blasted it out over the weekend and I didn't get anything." Start with about 3,000 at a time, or even fewer. In some cases, you might only want to do 1,000 at a time. The important thing is to get statistically reliable results.

Use a separate website

I'll say it again — integrating your lead generation process into your main corporate website is sheer lunacy.

When you do lead generation you want the prospect to stay topic/problem-focused, and not jump to a conclusion when they see your domain name.

If someone sees yourregularcompany.com they might make a judgment that will cost you a click. If they see theirproblemandsomegoodsolutions.com they are much more likely to respond.

But the dirty underbelly of lead generation (and I wouldn't be conscientious if I didn't warn you about this) reveals a series of problems than can befall you if you use your own domain:

1. Somebody inadvertently sends you a virus. On a separate website it goes no further; on your main website it can ball up your email for the next 3 days.

2. Three people on your 50,000 person opt-in email list forget they opted in. They email your ISP that you're spamming. Your ISP shuts down your main site. No revenue (if a part of your business is online), and you spend three days of your time trying to get it reinstated. Oh… by the way, your email is shut down during this time as well — and nothing makes a business owner hurt more than seeing employees sitting on their hands because they've lost their primary form of contact with your clients.

3. The IT person insisted that hosting the site on the company domain would be "no problem," only to create weeks to months of schedule delay because of firewalls, security software, work schedules, etc.

So please make the small investment in a separate site — $20 to $40 per month will literally save you thousands of dollars and many unproductive hours.

It's strictly a temporary commitment. If cost or security become considerations, you can eventually move it all onto your own servers. But I've found you're better off starting with a separate website, learning how to do the system right, and then integrating with your main website later when some IT person catches you in a weakened state.

Buy a turnkey system

Frequently when I speak, I'm asked, "How much does an outside firm charge to get a basic lead generation system operational?"

My answer is, "About half!"

In my experience the average "don't know enough to do it well" business owner or entrepreneur will burn about twice as much cash getting a program going as they would by bringing in an expert.

Face it. Most smaller companies have little to no email lead generation on staff.

Usually the staff is stretched pretty thin. Since email marketing is a fairly new vehicle, lots of people are not getting maximum mileage out of what they're doing. They may be doing certain things well, but they're doing other things poorly, and they sometimes blame the entire system for being "ineffective."

This is where a neutral third party can be valuable.

Sometimes all it takes is a simple change here, a little tweak there. Improve the title of a white paper, rewrite the opening sentence of an email, suggest an alternative list — any of these things might make a big difference.

Hiring a consultant to rework your entire process can cost thousands. But you can also get one to "spot-check" or critique an area you suspect needs improvement.

Conclusion

Most marketing executives, business owners, entrepreneurs and good sales people can learn how to run a good email marketing system pretty quickly.

In fact, I often hear people say things like, "If I had known it was going to be this easy, I'd have done it a long time ago!"

This email process is a joint venture on steroids, and so once your system works and once you know you have a persuasion approach that works, you can deploy it across your platform.

This is something that you can do. You can start small and learn a lot and learn it very quickly. You get the immediate feedback: usually within twenty-four to forty-eight hours. It doesn't take long for the results to be obvious.

You also get feedback from the people you send emails to. They'll call you. They'll write to you saying "I liked this, I didn't like that." You'll know you struck a wrong note because your recipients will tell you.

The important thing is to begin. This is something that you can do.

Start with a small audience. Get a feel for it and then move it forward. You'll get to a point very quickly — three to six months — where you will be able to apply some of the more sophisticated techniques. That's when you can really ramp up.

Remember to focus on problems that your products or service solve, and begin your persuasion approach from that perspective.

Keep your powder dry. Don't be in a hurry to close. It's okay to send five to ten emails sometimes before you actually mention the product or service or nature of the solution that you're offering. Find that problem first. Find that one raw nerve and hit it over a period of time to bring some part of the audience to a fever pitch.

And if you're selling something, you want to talk to people who are at a fever pitch, and find them some type of solution.

A good email marketing system raises their temperature automatically and systematically.

And, done right, it puts you in the position to cure what ails them.

Claim Your Purchase Bonus Worth $ 215 ...

In addition to this book, your purchase entitles you to 3 improtant tools that will help make your business more succesful.

1. **12 Emergency Tips For Improving Response To Your Direct Mail or Direct Email Lead Generation Programs. Audio mp3 with Slides**

    If you've developed an e-mail campaign, designed a white paper, developed a new web page and aren't seeing the results you want, this CD can help. Most marketers throw the baby out with the bath water. With this CD you'll learn how to spruce up that program that isn't living up to your expectations. Don't start over, just tweak what you've got.

    Retail price $125

2. **7 Fatal Mistakes Senior Executives Make With Their Complex Sales Cycle ...And How You Can Avoid Them. Audio mp3**

    Because complex sales cycles are so tricky and individual, it is no wonder that senior executives have a hard time getting a handle on them. Often times their "vision" is obscured by days to day operations. The Churchill Method has identified 7 common mistakes most likely to mess up your sales cycle with concrete, action-oriented ideas than can help you avoid those mistakes.

    Price $65

3. **Sales & Marketing Diagnostic—A 12 factor, self-scoring spreadsheet that will help you identify the weaknesses in your sales and marketing.**

    The checklist helps you rate your own sales and marketing process with respect to the things that matter most when the economy turns sour. And keeps you from getting caught "flat-footed" when the turbulence hits. Run this periodically to keep yourself on track.

    Price $29

    Total $ 215.00

To claim your bonus go to http:www.churchillmethod.com/gifts.html.

No additional purchase required.

Index

Author Biography

About Winton Churchill

Winton has more than 25 years experience developing, planning, organizing, and executing sales and marketing programs targeted in markets with complex sales cycles.

He is the developer the Churchill Method™, a process for systematically building relationships with prospects who buy.

In addition, Winton has written and lectured on a broad range of information technology and Internet sales and marketing topics.

His opinions are frequently quoted in a variety of publications, including The Wall Street Journal, Marketing Sherpa, Inc. Magazine, SoftwareCEO, Sales & Marketing Management, and a number of industry related business, Internet, and software related publications.

He has been a key player in a number of successful growth-stage software companies. He was Vice President of Sales and Marketing for Contact International Corporation, Inc., the developers of ACT! software, the world's leading sales contact management software.

Prior to Contact International, he was Vice President of Marketing and OEM Sales for Spinnaker Corporation, the world's 10th largest supplier of PC software during his tenure.

In addition to Contact International he has been involved in a variety of senior sales and marketing roles for Apple Computer, Oracle Corporation, Sun Microsystems, Legato Systems, and Netfish Technologies (now IONA).

Winton is Past President of the South Bay Association of Chambers of Commerce. The SBACC serves 18 Chambers and more than 53,000 businesses in coastal Southern California.

For his efforts there, he received a Congressional Commendation at the national level, and high praise and formal recognition from the California State Legislature and the Mayor of Los Angeles for his work with the Aerospace/Defense and Intelligence Community.

His name is frequently a point of curiosity for his readers and audience members. For a more complete answer to your questions about that go to http://www.churchillmethod.com/name.html

Notes

Printed in the USA
CPSIA information can be obtained
at www.ICGtesting.com
JSHW082210140824
68134JS00014B/541